William Alfred Quayle

The Poet's Poet and Other Essays

William Alfred Quayle

The Poet's Poet and Other Essays

ISBN/EAN: 9783337777869

Printed in Europe, USA, Canada, Australia, Japan

Cover: Foto ©Thomas Meinert / pixelio.de

More available books at **www.hansebooks.com**

THE POET'S POET

AND

Other Essays

WILLIAM A. QUAYLE

THIRD EDITION

CINCINNATI: CURTS & JENNINGS
NEW YORK: EATON & MAINS
1897.

To claim a new message to literary folk would be presumptuous. And the author's self-justification for this volume is that of a lover. A lover's passion makes him voluble. The words herein set down are expressions of loves historical and literary. And if these studies shall stimulate affection for the men and works he loves, the author will rest content.

WM. A. QUAYLE.

CONTENTS.

	PAGE.
The Poet's Poet,	7
King Cromwell,	39
William the Great, of England,	80
The Greater English Elegies,	124
Soliloquies of Hamlet and Macbeth,	139
"The Ebb Tide,"	151
The Jew in Fiction,	167
Robert Burns,	201
The Psychology of Nathaniel Hawthorne,	217
Shakespeare's Women,	246
"The Deserted Village,"	265
George Eliot as Novelist,	273
"The Ring and the Book,"	292
Shylock and David as Interpreters of Life,	326
Poem: An Angel Came,	352

The Poet's Poet and Other Essays

The Poet's Poet

ROBERT BROWNING is the poet's poet. And it is a tonic to the soul to recall what sort of man he was. Robert Browning was himself a poem. Pure, virile, versatile, balanced, profound, erudite, unsullied with base desire or impure motive; in aspiration outsoaring eagles; in love beautiful as any idyl ever dreamed; with singleness of purpose to be a poet, a poet only; in amplitude of thought swinging across the world; in labors abundant beyond Shakespeare; in character Christian; in faith triumphant, and dwelling

"Nigh to heaven, and loved of loftiest stars,"—

these are set down as main truths which certify Robert Browning to be both poet and poem. And he is the poet's poet because he is a mine from whose exhaustless store generations of poets may dig treasure. He dealt in hints. His poems, says Lowell, "were germs of wholesome ferment for other minds." His utterances were seeds, a tree's bulk in an acorn's cup. Poets shall sit before him as painters before a Raphael, and drink inspiration which shall prove

> "A joy forever,
> Whose loveliness increases, and will never
> Pass into nothingness; but still will keep
> A bower quiet for us, and a sleep
> Full of sweet dreams and health and quiet breathing."

The genius of Browning is no more a subject for debate than the genius of Shakespeare. That contemporaries were so slow to appreciate his might is one of the enigmas of our generation. "Here was the greatest English poet since Shakespeare," says Edward Berdoe, "pouring out treasures of thought, and we would have none of him." But failure on our part to appreciate this gift of God makes nothing against his genius. Landor was right in saying:

> "Shakespeare is not our poet; but the world's.
> Therefore for him no speech! and brief for thee,
> Browning! Since Chaucer was alive and hale,
> No man hath walked along our roads with step
> So active, so inquiring eye, or tongue
> So varied in discourse."

Mabie was right: "Since Shakespeare, no maker of English verse has seen life on so many sides, entered into it with such intensity of sympathy and imagination, and pierced it to so many centers of its energy and motive."

Professor Corson was right: "Browning is the most like Shakespeare in his deep interest in human nature, in all its varieties of good and evil;" "and he has worked with a thought-and-passion capital greater than the combined thought-and-passion capital of the richest of his contemporaries."

Elizabeth Barrett Browning, who loved her poet and wrote, celebrative of that love, Sonnets from the Portuguese, has said:

"Thou hast thy calling to some palace floor,
  Most gracious singer of high poems.
  Unlike are we, unlike, O princely Heart!
  Unlike our uses and our destinies.
  Our ministering two angels look surprise
  On one another, as they strike athwart
  Their wings in passing. Thou, bethink thee, art
  A guest for queens to social pageantries
  With gazes from a hundred brighter eyes
  Than tears can ever make mine, to ply thy part,
  Of chief musician. What hast thou to do
  With looking from the lattice lights at me,
  A poor, tired, wandering singer?"

I repeat, I do no more argue the genius of Browning than the genius of Shakespeare.

Raise this question, What is Browning's weakness? And allow him to have blemishes. We render no service in denying truth. Such championship is treason. No artist is perfect. No poet can claim infallibility in technique. So allow he has faults, such as a lack of sense of proportion, involved thought and treatment, infelicitous captions, and apparent crudity of style.

Browning's lack of sense of proportion grows out of his surprising affluence of thought. He sees all, and will tell all. This is the fault of sunlight. It transcribes the whole landscape. It goes into details, forgets nothing. Have you seen a forest mirrored in the quiet of an autumn stream? Did the light forget anything? The sky, gray as a tired face, lay sleeping in the stream. The banks with violet leaves huddled together; with sumacs, stout color-bearers holding up their banners of flame which the morrow would tear to tatters; with broken branches lying where the wind had thrown them down and forgotten them; with a patch of grass still green, though all but covered with leaves whose beauty was a memory—the bank lay anchored in the stream like a boat. And the tall trees girt round with strength, defying storms, the lordly trunk, the graceful drooping of the swaying branches, the exquisite tracery of the maple bark, the clinging ivy whose blushes had not quite faded from the cheek—the trees in this dear woodland seemed rooted in the stream. And the light, rare painter, had forgotten nothing. Such vision had Browning, and would photograph the world. "This and this I saw," is what he tells you. He was seer. Nothing eludes him. What not to write was more a trouble to him than what to write. His genius needed narcotic, not stimulant. He sees so much, too much for artistic effect. His very genius was his hurt. Walt Whitman has no trouble about proportion. His ideas are scant as December leaves. Gray was an unusual artist, and experienced no difficulty in subordinating parts, because his poet's thought was as scantily furnished as a poor man's parlor. Thoughts were his trouble: while with Browning superabundance is the peril. Poe, genius and artist as he was, wrote his music in one key. One thought stands in the foreground of all his verse. But Browning? Thought, imagination, resources of poetry crowded his mind like an o'erfull fountain. His poems are a wilderness, in whose tangle of vine and undergrowth and trees you find your way hidden and hindered. The richness of the soil was the traveler's hindrance.

And his poems are involved. Scarcely one of them which would not bear the prelude of an explanatory note. They are dark rooms, needing a lifted curtain to discover the hidden wealth of statue and picture. In his poems we do not know where to begin. The handling is abstruse. The wealth of thought bewilders. We have lost the points of the compass. The movement is so involved, so unusual, as to appear a process of bewilderment. Tennyson keeps straight on. To follow the course of a stream is not easier than to follow him. Browning impresses us at first acquaintance as not so much taking a journey as going on a ramble. His flight is as of a bird to whose wing fatigue is unknown. Browning is mystifying. We never feel quite sure we have his meaning. He keeps somewhat back. Though in many of his poems, if a clue be furnished us, the central truth is plain: yet without that clue we walk in darkness. Consider the following poems: "Abt Vogler," "How it Strikes a Contemporary," "A Toccata of Galuppi's," "Andrea Del Sarto," "Fra Lippo Lippi," "Bishop Blougram's Apology," and even "Saul." Not to understand time, place, person, is to find yourself nonplused; but once understood, how intoxicating the poem is! The "Grammarian's Funeral" stirs pulse like a battle's shout and tumult. "Fra Lippo Lippi" is such a study of lust in relation to art as opens a new page of soul-life to our eyes. A "Toccata of Galuppi's" reincarnates the voluptuous life of Venice on the seas as not all history knows to do. "Abt Vogler" and "Andrea del Sarto" are studies in artist psychology; the one in sound, the other in color, from whose witchery we know not how to escape. "Saul," open as it appears, is intricate in movement. One of the great poems of the century, it always bewilders. In Browning you never can be sure of yourself. You have a haunting fear lest the meaning you attach is not the poet's meaning; and that he is covertly laughing at you. Still, this very uncertainty comes to be a supreme attraction. We do not drink from empty cups nor from dry springs. In reading this poetry, the thrill of discovery is on you. Each new perusal gives a new intent of the poem. You feel a navigator in uncharted seas. I will not thank you for fountains if I can drink them dry. I thank you for the exhaustless. And Browning tantalizes you: he will give you room, sea-room, and a boat, and cry, "Set sail!"

Browning's titles for his poems are infelicitous. Some of them are execrable. "Red Cotton Night-cap Country," "A Bean-stripe: also Apple-eating," "Prince Hohenstiel-Schwangau, Savior of Society." We rebel against these titles as we would grow outraged with a surly porter at a gate. There is art in naming poems; and there is something in a name. True, a name comes to be beautiful to us from association with the owner, just as a face does. Some common names are music because of those who bear them. Alfred Tennyson seems a rare name for a poet, as does Robert Browning; but presumptively it is because these men were poets of so great gifts. But some names are intrinsically sweet. It would be hard for a woman who bore the name of Mary not to be lovely. Shakespeare displayed art in naming his plays, but rarer art in naming his women. I think he never gave a woman an unlovely name. If she were foul at heart, he would give her this one property of beauty. Jessica, Miranda, Desdemona, Cordelia, Juliet, Ophelia, Imogen,—why, these names are essential music. And Tennyson is artist in choosing captions for his poems. Arden, Ulysses, Ænone, Vivien, Elaine, Enid, Guinevere,—these seem to me sweet as the sound of a lute at night. But Browning was careless of these things. Some of his poems are exquisitely named. "Evelyn Hope," "Cleon," "Death on the Desert," "Pheidippides," "Blot in the 'Scutcheon," "Luria," "Sordello,"—who could fault such captions? His women are often gracefully named; witness, Mildred, Pippa, Colombe, Michal, Palma, Pauline, Constance, Evelyn, and the like. But one thing is clear: he took no large pains with titles. He ought. The portico is something. Often his titles are like the poems, hints; more, they are riddles. But in the main the poems bear descriptive titles, and the poem when read justifies the title. Such are: "Pippa Passes," "In a Balcony," "In an Inn Album," "Pietro of Abano," "The Two Poets of Croisic," "In a Gondola;"

but I make no doubt that this carelessness in caption is responsible for many a reader turning away, leaving the poem unread.

And Browning's style of expression is objectionable. His verse is certified to be crude; and so in many instances it is. "Sordello" represents this literary opaqueness, as in a greater or less degree many other poems do. We must admit he is careless, ragged sometimes, slovenly often. Sometimes his verse is not poetry at all, as in "Mr. Sludge the Medium." Shakespeare, without a word of explanation, stepped out of poetry into prose: this Browning does; and the objection to be offered is that he does not label it prose. Stedman quotes with approval the estimate of a friend to this effect: "His work seems that of a grand intellect painfully striving for adequate use and expression, and never quite attaining either;" but I am not of those who concur in Stedman's judgment. Browning, as I read him, was not incapable of exquisite grace or music. When he elected to be, he was as musical as laughter. "Evelyn Hope" is idyllic in sweetness. "Meeting at Night" and "Parting at Morning" are beautiful as the love they celebrate. Nobody forgets the song in "Pippa

Passes;" and the words Henry sung under Mildred's window are exquisite as the faultless lyrics in "The Princess." Have you read many sweeter things than the lyric which introduces "The Two Poets of Croisic?"

> "Such a starved bank of moss
>   Till that May morn,
> Blue ran the flash across:
>   Violets were born.
>
> Sky—what a scowl of cloud
>   Till near and far,
> Ray on ray split the shroud:
>   Splendid, a star!
>
> World—how it walled about
>   Life with disgrace
> Till God's own smile came out:
>   That was thy face."

Passages by the score could be selected which would justify this claim. The closing of the Pope's monologue in "The Ring and the Book" is deathless music and deathless poetry. I think it evident, therefore, that if Browning was not always musical, it was not because his was not the musician's gift. Many of his lines are as noble as Marlowe's, and his lyrics as dainty as a child's singing in the sun.

I go further. In Robert Browning's style is a phenomenal conjoining of meter to thought. Perhaps no English poet has equaled him in this regard. While often not musical, he is at one with his theme. The meter in "The Pied Piper of Hamelin" dances like the children who followed the piper's music. "How They Brought the Good News from Ghent to Aix"—well, we can hear the drum-beat of the horses' hoofs as, with distended nostrils, with panting flanks and foam-flecked sides, they galloped toward the announcement at Aix. "Mr. Sludge" has for theme the exposure of a humbug; and the style, uncouth as it is, is adapted to the theme. The lawyer's arguments in "The Ring and the Book" are in cast of argument and style not less admirably adapted for what they were intended than Caponsacchi, Guido, Pompilia, or the Pope. I may illustrate my meaning lucidly from "Caliban upon Setebos." In no one of this poet's productions is the style more distorted. You seem walking over the marl of an extinct volcano. You can imagine nothing purporting to be poetry more wrenched and misshapen. But consider that in no one of his series of psychological studies is Browning's genius more incontestable than in "Caliban upon Setebos." Caliban in Shakespeare's portrait was little raised above the brute. He is Prospero's animal, cowed, mastered, but brutal and vindictive. Browning conceives this poor savage as a speculator in theology. He lies face downward in the slush bordering the sea. He looks downward, as if anybody could get a sight of God without looking upward! Caliban's notion of God must be of the murkiest. God is an overgrown Caliban, mayhap a greater Prospero. Caliban's ideas must be distorted: his expressions will also be tangled, irrelevant, shapeless. To me, "Caliban upon Setebos" appears a triumph of form as of debased psychology, which grows more astonishing each time I read it. So, then, our conclusion is, Browning's style is far from the crude and abnormal creation many imagine it; often rude, oftener musical or adapted in the highest artistic sense to the part it was to play.

Thus far we have considered Browning's faults. Our attitude has been negative; but criticism is not the art of finding fault as some suppose, but is rather the art of discriminative observation. Destruction is not criticism in any valid sense. The negative in it corresponds to the clearing away the débris preparatory to construction. So the critic's chief and nobler business is to discover merit, as a navigator, continent and sea. Criticism is constructive, and must never content itself with negative processes. To name the faults of Browning, as the faults of any man or poet, is an easy task, since they are apparent. Faults lie in plain sight, while the massive genius of him remains to be discovered. Fault-finding is a superficial business, but discriminative discovery of merit is a profound business. To dismiss Browning as a certain critic did, calling his poetry simply "Trash," is a crude but easy process. Let ours be the manlier method of allowing faults where faults exist, but making our chief concern to discover worth.

And what is Browning's strength? And this word is apt, seeing he was what he was. Browning is virile. We know it is a man's voice we hear. Allow his strength to be dimly outlined in the following enumeration: Fecundity; wealth of theme, knowledge, and thought; dramatic power; profound psychology; Christian attitude; and inspirational value.

Browning rivals all our great poets in his

affluence of creation. Corson says: "His is the largest body of poetry produced by any one poet in English literature." A river formed by innumerable rivulets among the hills—silvery threads which go afar and drink waters from mossy bank and dewdrop from the morning flowers—a river thus formed is beautiful, and its origin has all the grace of poetry; but a river spouting from a fountain, a river at the first, is thrilling as a storm at sea. There is *such* prodigality of power in Browning. The heavens hold the stars and the oceans, and are not full. This poet has like limitless capacity. He gave in spendthrift fashion, withholding nothing; yet are his powers not exhausted. He, as his own Sordello, was found dead, and death put stop to his music. But had he lived! We no more conceive his productiveness run dry than that of Shelley or Keats, though his life was the age of both. "The Ring and the Book" is epic in size, conception, and treatment. Stedman has rightly said of it: "Yet the thought, the vocabulary, the imagery, the wisdom, lavished upon this story would equip a score of ordinary writers, and place them beyond danger of neglect." His resources wring wonder from us as the mountains do.

Browning's wealth of theme, thought, and knowledge constitute the second ingredient of his genius. To sit at twilight and barely run over the titles of his poems, will make you query whether you have not inadvertently named some productions belonging to another. Such range of theme has not been approached by any other poet. Shakespeare has been distanced here. Browning seems an eagle which, winging flight above the world, saw all his shadow fell across. He is as at home in history as in his own garden. Nothing is foreign to him. The Orient, Greece, Mediævalism, and the nineteenth century are all his home paths. "Ferishtah's Fancies," "Balaustion's Adventure," "Filippo Baldinucci on the Privilege of Burial," "James Lee's Wife," "Ivan Ivanovitch," are themes taken from the world and the centuries. He is as much at home in Mediæval Italy as Dante. He is saturated with its history as a floating spar with the salt seas. Nor is it outline he grasps, but minutiæ. His knowledge is copious to the point of tediousness. He has gone into many fields; yet not as gleaner, but as reaper. Anachronism in the unessential there is with him as with Shakespeare, but anachronism of spirit there is not. He is the poet of early Christianity; witness, "Cleon" as the decadence of heathendom and philosophy, and "The Medical Experience of Karshish," and "Death in the Desert." He is poet of the Jew: "Saul," "Rabbi ben Ezra," "Jochanan Hakkadosh," "Holy-cross Day." He is the poet of Protestantism: "The Bishop Orders his Tomb," "Soliloquy of the Spanish Cloister," "The Heretic's Tragedy," "Christmas Eve," and "Easter Morning." He is the poet of music, none like him, as witness "Master Hugues of Saxe-Gotha," "Abt Vogler," "A Toccata of Galuppi's." He understood music in a profound fashion, as a study of these poems will testify. He is the poet of painting: "Pictor Ignotus," "Fra Lippo Lippi," "Andrea del Sarto." He is poet of history, as you may see: "Protus," "Strafford," "Luria," "Clive," "King Victor and King Charles." He is the poet of the heart, as testify "Colombe's Birthday," "A Soul's Tragedy," "In a Balcony," "Blot in a 'Scutcheon," "La Saisiaz." He is poet of the intellect: "Sordello" is the poet, "Paracelsus" is the student; and all he has written is interpenetrated by the largest intellectuality. And he is specially the poet of our own century. A stream will glass every form of bird or cloud which floats above it: so Browning glasses our century. Its profoundest life is what he handles: its profoundest problems he probes. He knows the questions of the centuries are the same; but that the age gives color to the immortal queries as cathedral windows to white light. So we may safely call Browning the profoundest philosopher of our era, and the exponent of its largest life. Even this imperfect statement will make plain that he is universal in theme and knowledge. Besides, in this treatment is nothing superficial. His thought digs deep. Who follows the movement of his sword must have a quick eye, and who gets not lost nor bewildered in following this poet must be possessed of an intellect singularly acute.

Browning is always dramatic, and has written the solitary great tragedies since Shakespeare. Burns is always lyric, Keats narrative, Wordsworth didactic, but Browning invariably dramatic. His instinct is the actor's. His lyrics, with few exceptions, are dialogues. He dubbed himself,

"Robert Browning, writer of plays."

And in such monologues as the Pope's in "The Ring and the Book," he carries on dialogue with himself. In this poet we are never spectators: we are participants. His narrative poem, "Flight of the Duchess," is practically dramatic as "Pippa Passes." The energies of a mighty age this poet preserved in dramas, which, while not adapted to the theater, are greatly adapted to the human soul. "In an Inn Album" is as black with hypocrisy as Iago. "In a Balcony" is steeped in love as Merchant of Venice. "Pippa Passes" is as graphic a study of conscience as Macbeth. "Blot in a 'Scutcheon" is tragic as Romeo and Juliet. "A Soul's Tragedy" is penetrative in insight into character as Hamlet's dissection of motive and character of King Claudius. "Colombe's Birthday" is as lovely a comedy as the Tempest. And as part of this dramatic equipment, mention humor. Nature mixes smiles and tears. Laughter is native to us as weeping. Mrs. Browning mentions how babes

"Smile in sleep when wondered at for smiling."

Humor imports laughter. Shakespeare was prince of humorists, as he was prince of poets; and there is ever a smile lurking in his eyes, even when they are filled with tears. Jack Falstaff is the merriest jester artist ever created. His braggart speech and impudent lying do us good as a medicine. He is Shakespeare's extravaganza; but in some form, humor is on every page. It stands close even to the grave. But Browning is no humorist to depict a Falstaff. His is rather the humor of Hamlet, biting as the night air on the midnight terrace of Elsinore. Browning is ironist. He will laugh, shame things out of the world as Cervantes did; for there is no arguing down laughter. "Mr. Sludge the Medium," if viewed as a piece of irony, is captivating. Had Stedman taken that view, he would not probably have excoriated this scene as he did. Browning deals in the grotesque. "Fra Lippo Lippi" is as shrewd humor as lives. Because the poet does not hold his sides in laughter, we are not to suppose he never cracks a joke. He is as a Scotchman who jests, but does not laugh. His humor is not rollicking like that of the king's fool; is not hilarious like Hosea Biglow, nor genial as in Charles Lamb; but neither is it saturnine as in Swift. Browning satirizes folly. He will show the ludicrousness of pretense and hypocrisies. "The Ring and the Book" is full of the most delicious humor. On the way from or to tragedy he will have folly make itself a laughing stock. "Up at a Villa," "Down in the City," are straightly funny, and "Holy-cross Day" is riotously grotesque,

Browning is psychologist. His theme is soul. He is not dealing with surfaces, but with the deeps. He works from within out; is no painter, but binds soul on the rack, and makes it tell its secrets. Study Browning always from this point of view, if you would comprehend him. Note you, he will take classic themes, but never to treat them as other poets do—give a look at their ravishing mythology. Bayard Taylor's "Hylas," Keats's "Hyperion," Swinburne's "Atalanta in Calydon," Tennyson's "Ulysses" and "Ænone," represent the current method, and bewitching it is; but Browning will pass the mythology element by unheeded, and supply a study of motive. What a study "Cleon" is! Look at his "Echetlos," the unnamed warrior of Marathon, or "Pheidippides," the annunciator of Marathon's victory. He looks not so much on the laughing waters of the seas as he sounds the depths. I know not any poet who attempts doing in psychological studies what Browning does. Caliban is a study in anthropomorphism bewilderingly great. "Bishop Blougram's Apology" is a study of an unexpected sort. "Experience of Karshish" is profound. "Death on a Desert" goes deep into the Christian consciousness. "Saul" is a march of majesty in its exegesis of man's life in its entirety. "The Statue and the Bust" is a weird, wonderful, and solitary study of soul hunger, and the teaching of the fable, if restricted to the author's moral, is signal:

> "And the sin I impute to each frustrate ghost
> Is the unlit lamp and the ungirt loin."

A flower blooms because the secret of bloom is at its heart. Blossom is native speech. Browning is as exactly natural because in him the life of the soul speaks. His exactitude of utterance grows on you. That one man could have thrown himself into so many souls, and have spoken their speech with never a failure of tone, is the marvel pre-eminent of Robert Browning. It is the heart he speaks for. The most intellectual of poets, he is yet because of deep insight into the soul the apostle of the heart. All life's fire burns hot in him: life as a whole shall be his theme. The purely intellectual will delight him like moonrise. "The Grammarian's Funeral" speaks for the scholar, as Tennyson's "Ulysses" for the warrior. Aspiration finds a voice in "Rudel to a Lady of Tripoli." In Emerson, the culturistic element has quenched the fire of poetry, so that his poems are gray ashes. In Matthew Arnold, poetry dried up, an exhausted fountain. With Browning, intellectuality, splendid as a midday sun, was found to be consonant with heart, which spake for the race of women and of men. Love has had few special pleaders like Robert Browning.

And he was distinctively religious. Mountain air is saturated with odors of the pine, but not more so than Browning's poetry with the Christian spirit. He is optimist, not because he is blind, but because he is Christian. He saw the hills beyond the hills. He has two horizons. He is rebel against mere matter. He is no agnostic. In a doubt age he was

"Very sure of God."

He was as a soldier in the midst of battle: unperturbed, even triumphant.

"God rules in his heaven,
All's right in the world,"

is what Pippa sings, and is the adequate expression of the Christian attitude. All he wrote was flooded with immortality, as a lake with silver when the moon is risen. Such a staff as "La Saisiaz" props weakness up as if it were a ship's mast we leaned upon.

> "I but open my eyes—and perfection, no more and no less,
> In the kind I imagined full fronts me, and God is seen God
> In the star, in the stone, in the flesh, in the soul, and the clod."

"Saul" is the philosophy of the Christian life. Tennyson is theist; Browning, Christ-ist. Christ is omnipresent in Robert Browning.

And Browning is an inspirer. The noblest form of literature is inspirational. Encyclopædia knowledge is primary and puissant in its way, but gropes along a narrow way. It lacks outlook. It is where a voice calls me to lift eyes from my common task that the voice becomes potential and useful. Wordsworth says of Milton's sonnet, "In his hand the thing became a trumpet."

And this characteristic must appear in all true poetry: it inspires. Nor must this uplift be translated with dull literality. It means much, and its fingers sweep many keys. A great idea startles, arouses by sheer majesty. From such comes intellectual uplift. To look at a thought, be it cold as the dreary North, is an inspiration not to be undervalued. Its labor is eventful in human life. A great thought, whatever its compass, must charm like the sound of a lover's lute. Some thoughts uplift by their beauty. Calm as evening, or full of life as a rippling, flashing tide breaking in music on the shore, with beauty for a possession, there is uplift for the soul. Some thoughts have elevation and catholicity, which upbear as the sea a vessel's bulk, seeming to touch every faculty of the soul, and possessing power of penetration and diffusion. This effect is indescribable, but perceptible and blessed. In such qualities lies inspirational value. I make high claim for Browning here. His verse is often as the hills he graphically describes,

"Short, sharp, broken like an old lion's cheek teeth:"

yet the thinker can but be inspired by the omnipresence of thought. Some, even much of his verse is as the verse of Edward Lear—having a profounder meaning than appears to a casual reader. Literary opaqueness is not to be construed as depth, but depth there may be despite literary opaqueness. Browning has both the one and the other. His poems grow on us as Nature does. No man can measure their full mass at once. There is always, I may say, the impression of an unsuspected reserve of power, thought, feeling, and beauty. One cares to reread, to go over and over, as he retraces a path in a fair woodland by a brook in autumn. Some of his poems seem huge boulders, flung to lie jagged and massive in their imperial strength: others the tenderest speech of an o'er tender heart; and others appear the stride of a conquering faith.

In poetry, the two high peaks of the Victorian era are Tennyson and Browning. These two are masters. Two men could not differ more in nature or technique. Each is a poet: each is great: each knows what strings have music in them. Neither is a Swinburne, whose poetry is mostly exoteric. They have the subtle, incommunicable insight compelling poetry, which seizes the faculties of the soul, and uses them as Apollo the reed he holds. Poetry with Tennyson is not mere form: it is essence. Perfect in metrical mechanism, the poet's thought is more perfect still. Tennyson and Browning are contemporaries fit to be intrusted with the destiny of the imperial English speech for half a century. These are poets, with the word underscored as words in a girl's letter. Tennyson's ear is as swift to detect a rhythmic inaccuracy as a musician to discover discord. He gives to his poetic thought a perfect setting. He will make thought and expression twin perfections. He will have the rhythmic bark to which he intrusts his thought to float as gently as the boat that bears sweet, dead Elaine into her lover's presence. Browning submerges, loses himself in his thought. He is as if intoxicated with his conception. He must catch the perishable, vanishing form of beauty, and hold it at whatever hazard. He is an artist who sees the day go to his burial with such impressive obsequies as that he feels himself frenzied lest he should lose one glorious recollection; and so his brush dashes color on the canvas with the mad haste of a Turner. He must hold the hastening glory. Browning has no eye for mere form; he ignores, despises it. He thinks the greater must master. He feels that the thought burning like a furnace within him will commend itself to men despite its setting. The gem with him is all: the setting is of lesser consequence. So, briefly, these men differ: but it is no purpose of mine to draw a comparison between them. They need reading, not comparing. Each in his hemisphere flames like Orion.

Aside from Shakespeare, I have read no poet who inspires as Browning. His versatility; his range of theme; his profound erudition; his faculty of making himself at home in every age; his ability to seize the salient points in soul experience; his delineations, acid yet apt as photography; his vision from which no spirit can hide its secrets; his evident joy in life as life; his unrest with the visible and tangible; and his firm grasp on the invisible and intangible, which gives them back to us the sure realities of human experience; the buoyancy of faith which sees doubts, but plumes flight to soar above them; his love, deep, abiding, tender; his manhood, unsullied and serene; his copiousness of genius and execution, which reminds us of the affluence that feeds the Rhine—these combine to make this poet in his work and in himself an inspiration. At many points he reminds us of Shakespeare.

At other points he has done larger things than this chief. Shakespeare is superior in delineating woman as a lover; but in her profoundest life—namely, religious vision, fidelity, and heroism—he is lacking. In not any of his women has he touched this splendid possibility. There are about him limitations, perhaps those of his century; but one rises from the contemplation of Shakespeare's women, first and last, with the sense of lack upon him. It is not so in Browning. He glasses woman's largest life. He misses no element of power, and in particular does he not miss the chief fact of soul. Shakespeare has no such woman as Pompilia; indeed, universal literature has not her like. She is the noblest female figure given us by creative genius. Browning has given us life-sized woman. She has a lover; but she has her babe and her God. The lover as in Miranda and Jessica, the wife as in Imogen and Desdemona—are adequate; but Shakespeare has scarcely given us an ideal mother, while woman, the devotee of duty, is hinted in Cordelia; and woman, the worshiper, is not so much as mentioned. Hamlet is the profoundest study literature has produced of the soul longing for divine verities; but Hamlet has no counterpart in Shakespeare's women. But Pompilia might pass for Hamlet's sister, save that she sees God, while Hamlet died groping for the curtain, and not even with convulsive dying grasp pulled it from between God's face and him.

In Browning, we feel adequacy of treatment, from which comes inspiration. No one can be inspired, except under the sense of a deed adequately performed. When in history or fiction we behold a heroism, we rise from the study inspired because the character measured up to the occasion. For this reason, Hall Caine's Red Jason, Dickens's Sidney Carton, Thackeray's Henry Esmond, Hugo's Jean Valjean, Tennyson's King Arthur, take the soul by storm. And Browning is adequate. "The Ring and the Book," "Pippa Passes," "Blot in the 'Scutcheon," "La Saisiaz," "The Grammarian's Funeral," and "Saul" burn themselves in the soul, because we feel them equal to the occasion. The artist executed the task he undertook. Genius and task were met. In reading, two phases of inspirational value present themselves—the fragmentary and the entire. Some authors excel in splinters of inspiration. Such works lend themselves easily to an anthology. Shakespeare has some plays specially rich in quotable passages of beauty, excerptible patches of sunlight. Richard II and Merchant of Venice have many such; but the value of the whole is not in necessary ratio to the value of these fragments. In other Shakespearean plays there are few distinct, isolated beauties, while the whole makes a living majesty. Tennyson abounds in passages of beauty so rare that one finds it all but impossible to go on with the reading. He is as a traveler who, on the way to some vantage ground of vision, finds himself hindered or halted at every step by reiterated beauties. Who that marks passages of special loveliness does not find "Idyls of the King" one continuous marginal annotation? But in the main the chief afflatus of "Paradise Lost" springs from the mass of that imposing epic. Some poems inspire us like the bulk of a mountain; we forget the separate elements, lost in presence of the whole. Now, Browning is inspiring for both causes mentioned. Irregular he is; but it is never well to sleep while reading him; for, when least you think it, he will reward your waking with an apocalypse. Who sleeps when journeying through Switzerland? But I would feel less loss were mine in such a slumber than to drowse while passing over a tract of Browning's poetry. In him, the whole always throws its shadow across the path. I know not one of his poems which does not leave some thought or question insistent in the mind. Treasures worth a king's ransom are here. He is full of beauty like the spring, and big with elevation. I account it one of life's rare delights to go aside with this Christian prophet. He girds me with strength. In his company (to use his own words) I am

"Stung with the splendor of a sudden thought,"

and feel

"Why stay we on the earth except to grow?"

And viewing Robert Browning, the poet's poet, as we would view a mountain we had climbed, what truer and more gracious words for the expression of our thought than these borrowed from Keats's immortal sonnet?

"Then felt I like some watcher of the skies
  When a new planet swims into his ken;
Or like stout Cortes when, with eagle eyes,
  He stared at the Pacific."

King Cromwell

FELLOWSHIP with great ideas amplifies the soul. The study of a sunset or a mountain or the sea exalts him who studies. Great ideas are the heritage of the human mind. But a man is always greater than any material thing. The spiritual always dwarfs the physical. The mountain, lifting forehead to the heavens, is less a giant than the man who stands at its far base and computes its altitude. The locomotive, with its ponderous complexity, is simplicity and commonplaceness as compared with Stephenson, who created the iron monster and governs its goings. The ocean, that home of slumbering storms and wrathful tempests, that symbol of infinity and omnipotence,—the ocean is not so great as the dreamy man who stands upon its shore and meditates its mastery. Columbus is greater than the great Atlantic.

A man is an aggregation of ideas. He embodies some movement; is the amplification of some concept. He is, therefore, of supreme importance to the world. He is, by virtue of his greatness, passed into the circulating medium of the intellectual realm, and is not to be underrated. To study him is not servility nor hero worship, but is wisdom and honest dealing with one's own life. Show me greatness, and you have made me your debtor. To be associated with the colossal elevates the spirit. This is a common fact of intellectual history. Every man who has lifted himself from the low levels, where he found his life groveling, knows that except he had touched the hem of greatness' garment, he had never arisen even to his little height.

Cromwell was a great soul. Near him I feel as if I stood within the shadow of a pyramid. The day is gone when men wrangled over his greatness. If any man call the roll of imperial genius, be sure the name of Oliver Cromwell will be there. His burly figure stalks across every stage where genius doth appear. There are some men who are locally great. Their genius is provincial. They belong to vicinities. Close at hand they seem men of mighty stature; far removed they appear as pigmies on the plain. To this class most men of note belong. They have their day. They serve their generation. Their service to the world is not to be underrated. Without them history would indeed suffer loss. And yet their speech is not a world speech, nor are they world figures.

There are other men who have no marks of provincialism, either in speech or look. They have hung their blazing orbs so high as to have become the luminaries of the world. Their glory is so illustrious that all men count them stars of the first magnitude. They have "become a name." The earth esteems their fame a precious heritage. To this decimated list the name of Cromwell belongs. However much men differ in their estimates of his character, there is practically no differing on the question of his genius. There is a unanimity of sentiment here, which must strike every reader of biography and history with delighted surprise.

Gladstone ranks Cromwell with Charlemagne and Napoleon. Clarendon recognizes him as no common man. Nicholson says: "He was a man for all ages to admire, for all Britons to honor in proud remembrance;" and adds: "No royal name, at least since Alfred's, is more worthy of our veneration than that of the usurper, Oliver Cromwell." Thurloe,

Cromwell's Secretary of State, himself no mean figure, declares, "A greater soul never dwelt among men." Goldwin Smith says, "A greater proof of practical capacity was never given." Macaulay calls him "the most profound politician of his age," and says: "Such was his genius and resolution that he was able to overpower and crush everything that crossed his path, and to make himself more absolute master of his country than any of her legitimate kings had been." Cardinal Mazarin gave his grudging but incontestable testimony to the Protector's greatness, in that he "feared Cromwell more than he feared the devil, and changed color at the mention of his name." The above remark will have the more significance if it be remembered that the cardinal had a lively belief in a personal devil; and his life was such that it can not be doubted he had a wholesome fear of him. Guizot, who can not be classed among Cromwell's panegyrists, pays this tribute to him: "He is, perhaps, the only example which history affords of one man having governed the most opposite events, and proved sufficient for the most various destinies." This list of testimonials to the greatness of the man Cromwell may well close with the phrase of Carlyle. To him, among his heroes, he is "Great Cromwell." And, indeed, there is no assignable reason why this man should not be placed in the list with a Great Frederick and a Great Charles. By right of his genius, he may well be named Cromwell the Great.

If I am told that the man about to come upon the stage is one who founded empires, wore a crown of more than royal splendor, won plaudits from unwilling lips—and if such a man come, can it be otherwise than that I shall view him with attentive vision, even with my soul in my eyes! Behold, Cromwell is here!

He is five feet ten inches high. He is broad, burly, and half-clad in mail. A huge head, "fit to be the workshop of vast matters," is planted on his shoulders. He is fiery, fierce, brave as Achilles, yet tender as a woman. His is an English face. No perfumed Adonis he; no fine-cut Greek features—a Briton all and all. No man can well mistake this man's nationality. He looks of the race which produced him; eyes that look into things and beyond them; silent, melancholic, fitted for a soldier in a world's battle. He seemed a tower which it were folly to attempt to storm; a bolt shot from a thunder-cloud, impossible to resist; a sphinx riddle, no man could solve; a secret that must die untold; a man you would turn to look upon when you pass, not knowing why you looked. The Puritan soldier and prince has come. Look!

Cromwell was born in 1599. As Carlyle has finely said, he was "always a year older than his century." Four years later, Elizabeth died, and the Tudors were but a name in history. He was born during a lull in national affairs, which was the calm before the fury-burst of the tempest. His life began on the verge of such a precipice that "the murmuring surge that on the unnumbered idle pebbles chafes, could not be heard so high"—a sheer leap down into a seething sea of war, of anarchy, of blood. His life was an arch which spans the chasm between two dynasties. History has shown that he lived in a crisis, and was a man born for crucial moments in the chemistry of nations. Some men are fitted for epoch making—sinewy to withstand the fury of tremendous onset. Athanasius, Savonarola, Luther, Cromwell, Pym, Lincoln—these men seem molded in colossal matrices for unusual service and superior destinies.

Cromwell was well born; not greatly born. Here is a wise distinction nature makes, and men might well mark. He was not plebeian, was not prince. The blood of Scotch royalty flowed through his veins, and the strength of English yeomanry was latent in his arm. Through and through, he was a representative of the land of his nativity. He was of the middle rank, which has made England what England is. He was a farmer, a cattle-breeder, a soldier cast in nobler than Roman mold. He was a man of college training, by forecast a lawyer: by providence and fealty to duty, a farmer, a general, a statesman, a king.

Every man's genius is colored by his age. His environment does not control, but does put its stamp upon his destiny. The image and superscription of genius is imprinted by the age which produces the man. Few men are to be understood apart from their times. We must study the topography of genius, if we would comprehend the achievements of generals and the utterances of kings. If you will rehearse to me the story of Prometheus, tell me not only his name and fame, but that a black, scarred crag of the Caucasus held him, that the vultures gnawed at his vitals, that lightnings hurled their gleaming spears about his head, and thunders made his lonely citadel of pain to rock like fisher's bark on tempest-drenched seas. These things, the dire accessories of woe, are necessities for the comprehension of the Titan tale. So of Moses, I must know not only who, but where: Egypt, born of a slave, adopted by a queen, learned in all the knowledge of that wisest land, a king's heir, self-exiled from the throne, lone Midian with its wandering flock, the sea passed through dry-shod, the desert, Sinai, the law, Pisgah, Nebo—all these things must be told ere I can comprehend the life of the chiefest legislator of the world.

So must I understand the times in which this man Cromwell wrought if I would comprehend his achievements. Born in Elizabeth's reign! What a heyday of glory! What glamour clings about those days! Chivalry, romance, Raleigh, Leicester, din of arms, shout of victory, crash of Armadas, and through all haughty-faced, golden-haired Elizabeth, standing an omnipresent personality!

How these incongruities become congruous when seen in those historic times! But we must look into these things more narrowly. Students of history must look through appearances into realities. Elizabeth's age was an age of incomplete reformation, of decaying chivalry, of commerce and colonization, of surprising energy and action, which produced the drama. These points summarize the distinctive features of the Elizabethan era. Look at them briefly.

The Reformation had no stronger or more virulent opposer than Henry VIII. He loved a woman not his wife, and wished to divorce his queen. Rome would not grant the king's desire, whereupon Henry denied Papal supremacy. He married Annie Boleyn, and introduced the Reformation; but such a distorted semblance as to be scarcely recognizable. The Reformation came to England to gratify the lust of a lecherous king. The new Church differed from the old in one regard. In the old, the Pope was supreme; in the new, the king was supreme. King and Pope were combined in a single person. Here was the union of Church and State. It must be apparent that a change made for such reasons and continued under such forms, must be a thing from which pure men would revolt. Elizabeth sustained the same relation to the Church as had her father. With her the Church was a subordinate department of State. She was Protestant by circumstances. Her conscience was no active member of the Royal Council. She was head of the Protestant powers of Europe more as a matter of policy than religion. Indeed, to speak with even reasonable accuracy, she was such solely for politic reasons. It was, let us say sadly but with all certainty, an era of incomplete Reformation.

It was also an age of decaying chivalry. The day of chivalry was growing late. The purity of knighthood was largely a departed glory. Instead of the nobility of sincerity, which made beautiful the face and fame of King Arthur, there was the laugh of insincerity and the hollowness of hypocrisy. Chivalry was a dying splendor. The Sidneys and Raleighs were a hopeless minority. The impurity that blights was rife. The court of Elizabeth was not the home of a Christian queen. The captivating beauty of Spenser's "Fairie Queen" finds no counterpart in the chivalry of Elizabeth's reign. "False Duessa" of Spenser's tale might well stand as the sad symbol of Elizabethan chivalry. Elizabeth fostered hypocrisy. She watered with her woman's hand that upas tree. She smiled on knighthood kneeling at her throne, with lies as black as treason on the knight's lips. Chivalry, with its storied purity, was not. The Crusader, whose heart was full of nobility, and whose hand was full of deeds of high emprise, was dead. He slumbered in his grave; and with him slept the sacred dust of Christian chivalry.

This was an age of discovery and colonization. The English were beginning to guess the secret of their insular position. The sea was beckoning them to sail beyond the sunset. The fire that burned within the life of the Renaissance burned here. Men urged their way along the yeasting seas; they longed to sight new worlds. A Columbus heart throbbed in many a discoverer's breast. They sought new lands; and new lands found must be peopled. Commerce must build her metropolis of trade. Sailors, soldiers, settlers, must go together. These were contemporaries in the new land. Boldness characterized the adventurer in

Elizabeth's reign. She herself was as brave as Boadicea. Cowardice is not one of Elizabeth's sins, nor is it a sin of her age. There were bold men in those days, and they sailed to the world's limit, and essayed to seize new hemispheres for England's supremacy.

It was the age of the drama. Those were days of action. Tremendous and almost resistless energy was here. The blood ran like lightning along men's veins. Magnificent energies were driving along like a whirlwind. It was an actor's age. The drama grew out of the nature of things. That species of poetry grew in Greece when Athens was as sleepless as the ocean. It is the exponent of superlative energy. In such an atmosphere the drama grows to its full height. In Elizabeth's reign the drama "rose like an exhalation." In a brief period it grew to such noble proportions that it might well lay claim to have wrested the scepter from the hand of Attica. Elizabeth's age shows the drama at its best; since then it has declined, a setting star.

In an age marked with such peculiarities, Cromwell was born. Elizabeth's was essentially a feudal reign. The Tudors were a feudal house. Elizabeth was a feudal sovereign. She, hating death, died. Death tore the scepter from her hand, the purple from her shoulders, the crown from her head; he took her from her throne, and hewed her out a tomb. The Tudors were dead; the Stuarts were come. Strength was no more. Weakness clung with timid fingers to the royal prerogatives. In 1603, Elizabeth lay dying; in 1649, Charles Stuart's head dropped on the scaffold at Whitehall—in 1603, a whole people delirious with loyalty; in 1649, all England sullen with wrath that slew their king. Truly, "the old order changes, giving place to new." But the change in appearance was only indicative of the change the people had undergone. It was a tide telling how high the sea had risen. We may well challenge history to show so radical a change in so brief a period. It was the sailing into a new, untried sea. It was the passing into a new hemisphere lit with new stars; into a realm unknown, vast, curtained with mystery. It was a change so entire, so unparalleled, that no precedent could be adduced. It was sailing when chart and compass and stars are gone.

This was not the England of Elizabeth, but a new and untried thing. Hers was the England of the cavalier and the Churchman. This was the England of the commoner and the Puritan. It resembled the old order only in its possession of tremendous and resistless energy. The river still plunged like a mountain torrent toward the sea; but the channels were changed. Puritanism was here. It came like an apparition. It stalked upon the stage of human affairs, and men knew not whence it came, nor whither it hastened. It was a strange thing; it was a great thing. What, then, is Puritanism? This question needs candid answer. More, it demands it. Puritanism is not an incomprehensible thing, but is in the main an uncomprehended thing. Men laugh at it, make their common jests at its expense. I had as lief laugh at Niagara or the Matterhorn. Stupendousness is not a fit subject for jest, nor sublimity a theme fitting the humorist's powers; yet the greater part of men's knowledge of Puritanism is that which appertains to its vagaries. It had idiosyncrasies; all greatness has. It was not perfect, but was such a thing as towered immeasurably above all religious contemporaries. In our day, looking back across that seventeenth century plain crowded with armies, misted with battle-smoke, tumultuous with battle's din—

looking back we behold Puritanism a peak lifting itself so high into the azure that, when all else is hid, it stands sublime, a beacon to the world. Puritanism was no tangle of incongruities, no maze of absurdities. It was wise above its day. It was a revolt against falseness, hollowness, hypocrisy. It was an exodus of men from an Egypt of falsehood and insincerity into a Canaan of truth. It was the coming to the side of truth; the taking stand within the ranks of God.

As has been shown, the Anglican Church was half Romanism and more. It lacked those elements which should characterize an ecclesiasticism. From such a thing the Puritans departed; and never had a religious exodus more justification. Puritanism was an incarnation of Christian conscience. That is saying much, but is speaking noble truth. True, it was not the genial and beautiful thing Christ's manhood was. They patterned rather after Moses and Elijah than after Christ. But better Moses than Pharaoh, better Elijah than Ahab. Those who can scarcely marshal words meet for the task of condemning the Puritan severity of morals and life, find no difficulty in passing the orgies of a brothel court of the second

Charles with a feeble and smiling condemnation that amounts to a magnificat of sin. It were well to preserve at least a semblance of fairness in discussing important matters. So Puritanism came. It asked no man's leave. It stood a stern, strong, heroic thing. It championed the cause of purity and devotion to God. It believed in the brotherhood and common equality of man. It believed in one God and one Book. No better and no nobler tribute can be paid that band of Christian men and women whom history names Puritans than to say, as has been said, "They were men of one Book." The Bible was their *vade mecum*. These men possessed a devotion to duty, as they apprehended it, which was as beautiful as a mother's self-sacrifice; stern and pitiless as the winter's storm toward Romanism and sin in any guise, but tender towards wife, mother, babe, as any heart that ever beat. They were knights in a new and illustrious chivalry. They made battle for purity of thought, lips, and life. My heart, as it beholds the Puritan, cries, "Hail, all hail!"

This change was great past all belief. Pray, you, what caused it? But one answer is possible,—the Bible. The Bible is a revolutionizer. That was *the* Book. Puritanism pored over it as schoolboys con their lessons with bent heads. They were saturated with the Bible thought and Bible phrase. Their thought framed itself to speech in the Bible sentences. On Dunbar's field, when mists began to lift and the battle came, Puritan Cromwell cried, "Let God arise, and let his enemies be scattered." His was the Puritan speech. His life was molded by God's Book. With it all Puritans held constant companionship. The Bible is a renovator. Let the Bible enter any man's thought, and it will ennoble. Stand a man face to face with the Bible concepts, and he will begin to pant for room. It flings vastness into his soul. The Bible begets a new life. Puritanism was new. Men thought these men monstrosities; but they were noble normalities. There were in them greatness, wisdom, goodness. Looking at them, we say, scarcely thinking what we utter, "There were giants in those days."

Cromwell was a Puritan. He was permeated with the decrees. His was a bilious temperament. He was moody, silent, brooding, melancholy. All great souls have melancholy hours, and know the ministry of silence.

Moses prepared for God's work in the solitudes of Horeb; and every Moses must be girt for his great battles by the ministration of sublime silences. Cromwell, in his fen lands, in his silence, mused on God's Word, was converted, came into the secret of the Divine, merged his life into the life of God, and came to be a moody soul lit with resplendent Bible lights. Who does not comprehend this will not comprehend Cromwell. The hieroglyphics of this man's life are not decipherable if a man holds not this key. He embodied Puritanism. To know Milton and Cromwell is to know Puritanism. They are the high tides of that illustrious era. Cromwell had seen false chivalry die; had seen the true chivalry spring into majestic life; had seen the Puritan day grow crimson with the dawn. He dwelt under Stuart tyranny. That family was weak. The Tudors, whatever their faults—and they were many—were strong. Henry VII had a giant's arm. He was of kingly stature and imperial mold. Henry VIII, libertine as he was, had kingly powers and talent for administration akin to genius. Even Mary, with her hands dyed in martyr's blood, was not weak. She had virility not wholly mastered by her woman's heart. Her successor might well be named King Elizabeth. She was king, not queen. And when the government passed from a royal line, whose powers and prowess were manifest, into the hands of driveling incompetency and pedantic weakness, the antithesis was so startling as to waken men from their quiescent moods, till on the lips of even steadfast loyalty there came the unpremeditated query, "Why should this weakness reign over us?"

Men will forgive much if there be strength. The French tolerated a Louis XIV, and not a Louis XVI, because the one was strong, and the other weak. They tolerated the administration and gloried in the rule of a Napoleon, and dethroned a Charles X, because Napoleon, though a tyrant, was strong; and Charles was a tyrant and weak. The Stuarts were weak. There was no strength among them. Charles II, in spite of his monstrous vices, had more of the symptoms of strength than James I, Charles I, or James II. James I was a pedant, an overgrown schoolboy, "the wisest fool in Christendom." Charles I was the creature of favorites, was possessed of no gift of comprehending the people whom he ruled, was an egotist, and as false as even a king could well be. James II was an intolerant bigot, blind as a mole, and so incapable of learning that even a scaffold dyed with his father's blood could teach him no wisdom. Such were the Stuarts. The Tudors had been tyrannical, but were not pusillanimous in their weakness. There was no more despotism in James I than Elizabeth, nor in Charles I than in Henry VIII; but there was strength in the Tudors, and only weakness in the Stuarts. They were a puerile race. Charles had all the Tudor's pride and self-assurance, with none of the Tudor's astuteness or strength; and the result is what any attentive reader of history might forecast. Men rebelled. The Puritan revolution grew as naturally as ever did the wind-flower or the violet.

Liberty is a perennial reappearance. When man thinks it dead, it but "mews its mighty youth." It marches forward and upward. The contest between cavalier and Puritan was liberty's conflict. The battle belonged, not to England, but to the world. It was the cause of our common humanity. And Cromwell, as the leader in the fray, becomes a figure in liberty's lists, and a character of consequence in the history of men. To every lover of liberty the name of Oliver Cromwell must have in it a deep and solemn music, like the singing of a psalm. Liberty's battle is on. The King is uppermost. He is victorious. Capacity comes to the front. Cromwell moves into view. He was no seeker of place; place sought him. He tarried at home, and did the work that came to hand. He hated oppression. He loved liberty. What his kinsman Hampden did in the matter of ship-money, that Cromwell did in the matter of the draining of the fens. He felt himself in a high sense a subject of the government of God. He held himself ready to move obedient to the Divine command. Where duty called, he followed. Liberty called Cromwell: he did not call himself. The exigencies of the hour pronounced his name. Capacity makes room for itself. It is always so. Gustavus Adolphus came because the place needed him. In the swirl of battle great men appear, because the time calls them. When liberty puts clarion trumpet to her lips, and sounds her note of wild alarm, then a host answers, "Lo, we come." War came in a great nation. This was no race of warriors, and had no long list of military greatness from which to call leaders. The time came when the nation's life hung by a thread; when freedom's empire was well-nigh lost; and in the time of dire extremity help came. Grant, the invincible, with unostentatious bearing, comes and leads a million men to victory. It was the triumph of capacity. Greatness needs no herald before its face, nor asks for place, gift of another's hand; but does its duty, bides its time. So Cromwell came; illustrious day! He saw what others did not see. This battle was not primarily between social classes, but between conscience, religion, manhood on the one hand, and no conscience and hollow insincerity on the other.

"We must have God-fearing men," said Cromwell. This was a speech genius alone could pronounce. That was insight into the very spirit of the times. He knew the thing with which he had to cope. What his coadjutors took years to learn, his acumen discovered at the first. Others led, he followed. Others in the van, he in the rear. He was not troubled about notice or praise. "God noticed him," says Carlyle. He was so faithful to his God and the cause of liberty as an inferior, as to be felt the superior of all.

King Cromwell

Some men seem great by lack of standard of measurement. Among a race of Lilliputians, a Gulliver becomes a giant. In inferior epochs, a man may tower above his contemporaries; not because he is so great, but because they are so insignificant. It is possibly so in this instance. But the question need not delay for answer. Look at his contemporaries. Call the names of those men who made those times memorable: Elliot, Pym, Hampden, Milton, Ireton, Thurloe, Blake,—this is a roll of greatness. These men would have shone in the constellations of any age. Add the name of Strafford, that imperious aristocrat, the statesman of the first Stuart reign, and we shall find that Cromwell lived among men whom the world reckons great. How then came this Cromwell to stand among them so vast? If the man was not fit figure for the world's Pantheon, there is no explanation for the fact. He was a leader. He rose from the level where he served his country, to where he was the cynosure of every eye and the desire of England. He hid himself. He put others forward. He asked no rank, but seemed lost in the cause of freedom.

It is observable that in some eras great men

multiply. The times demand greatness. No progress is possible, except nature do bestir herself. See what hosts of notable generals the French Revolution produced. The names of men of superior powers in the American Revolutionary period are legion. It was the same in the crisis of the Rebellion. It is in such times, as if to meet the rush of the tempest and to withstand the mad charge of the sea, one gathered the latent, unsuspected energies of his manhood, and dedicated them every one to the task of standing impregnable as a tower. In this struggle for liberty, when great issues hung in the balance, greatness multiplied. Statesmen unknown arose, and did legislate for generations that were yet to be. The call, the answer, were blended in one voice. Great men were clustering about the standards of liberty; and the most commanding figure on this stormy field is Oliver Cromwell. He is not to be accounted great because he dwelt among a pigmy brood; but rather that, among a coterie of men whose talent was far removed from mediocrity, he, Saul-like, towered a head above them all. Essex must go to the rear; not that Cromwell willed or planned it, but that a greater than he had come. Cromwell desired Fairfax to have command of the war against the Scots; England had other desires. She knew the general for the conduct of this war was not Fairfax, but Cromwell. The nation had come to know its leader, and Dunbar and Worcester justified England's choice. This quiet, unassuming man now stands revealed,

"The pillar of a people's hope,
The center of a world's desire."

He "came, saw, conquered." He massed his God-fearing, praying battalions, and flung them on his enemies like an avalanche. God-fearing men led by a man of God were invincible. The world looked and wondered. Battle with these men was duty; for they fought God's battles. Cromwell suspected he was there to win.

He declared he would slay the king, should they meet in hour of conflict. He knew his era as no other knew it. He conquered the king, the Irish, the Scotch, the Parliament. He merits the name of Cromwell the Conqueror. The train of his victories is like a silver highway on the swelling sea when the great moon is full.

It is not possible in a brief sketch to give an adequate estimate of genius such as this man possessed. For such task volumes only can suffice. But the characteristics of the man may be summed up best under a dual heading: First, the accusations brought against him; second, the claims made for him. Under the former of these captions three indictments may be mentioned: He was a hypocrite; he was cruel; he betrayed the cause of liberty.

These are grievous charges. They do not militate against his genius; but they, if provable, will blast his character like an eternal mildew. Note each accusation. But before that task be attempted, let it be remarked that his contemporary biographers were those whom he had conquered in battle or mastered in diplomacy. They wrote with pen dipped in gall. Suppose the solitary biographer of the Christ had been Annas or Caiaphas, Sadducee or Pharisee, what distorted features of the Lord would we behold! It is but too apparent that, as seen through their eyes, he would have looked the embodiment of iconoclasm, self-opinionation, and colossal arrogancy. We have other, truer, and therefore fairer pictures. They who loved him spoke of him as he was. They who hated him had caricatured him, and written beneath the travesty, "This fellow." Cromwell's life was not written by men who knew and loved him, but by defeated cavaliers, by jealous inferiority, wrathful because of the man's supremacy, or by lovers of liberty who were dreamers, and had not the insight to discern what Cromwell perceived. With such biographers, who can wonder that the Cromwell of history seems a monster, a second Nero, whose memory is fit only for obloquy? This word of warning is absolutely necessary for those who would know the Puritan general and statesman aright.

To the charge of hypocrisy let it be replied, while his enemies are a unit in this accusation, they are not at all agreed as to the particular instances in which his omnipresent hypocrisy was displayed. One says he was profoundly hypocritical in advocating Fairfax's leadership in the war against the Scots; while Mrs. Harrison is sure that, though he was a monster of duplicity, he was honest here. Cromwell was not a hypocrite. If he was a hypocrite, then was a towering genius exercised here as elsewhere. Hypocrisy is acting a part, wearing a mask. Cromwell, if he wore a mask, never dropped it. Not in word spoken or written, not in public, nor in privacy to his best beloved, did he seem other than we know him. We are told his religious phrases were a hypocrite's cant; but if any man can candidly read his letters and speeches and so believe, I marvel at his insight. What I maintain is that, if the man was a hypocrite, he was the most masterful deceiver history portrays; he was genius in his craft. In truth, the man was the soul of honest intention. He was a believer in God and the Puritan cause, and in his own mission. He thought himself called of God to act his heroic part. He was a believer in Divine decrees. He prayed, agonized, came from his hours of introspection, imbued with the idea of God's commission for a given task. Such a view of Cromwell makes his life rational. We can thus comprehend it. There is logical consecutiveness in his character. But on any other theory there is no clue whereby to escape the labyrinth. The charge of hypocrisy is an easy method of explaining an abstruse human problem. It is a method much in vogue for explaining what otherwise is inexplicable. In my judgment there is no shred of proof of Cromwell's alleged hypocrisy.

"Cromwell was cruel." I incline to the opinion that this will not bear the light of honest investigation. He was stern; he was a Puritan. That character was modeled after the Old Testament, rather than the New. The severity of Moses with the Amalekites was before Cromwell's eyes. Those heathen, to his thought, were not more assuredly the enemies of God than the men against whom the Puritan unsheathed his sword. The instance always adduced as proof positive of this charge is the massacre of Drogheda and Wexford. But certain facts must be noted. War is not among the amenities. It is always cruel. But in this epoch, war was clothed with horrors our century can not comprehend. Tilly, in the Thirty Years' War, had been guilty of the most execrable atrocities. The Catholics in Ireland, during the early stages of the Parliamentary struggle, had massacred helpless victims with such savage cruelty that England looked upon the perpetrators as fiends incarnate. They were savage belligerents, whose proclivities for slaughter were so well known that it seemed essential to fling an abiding terror into their hearts. This was the end in view when Drogheda and Wexford were stormed, and their population slaughtered. The end was gained. The hostile Irish were so totally subdued by the severity that they were guilty of no further outrage. Cromwell's plan, when the whole scope of affairs is considered, was without question the kindliest which could have been devised. This man by nature was not cruel. His government was not one of fierce acerbity. His was a gentleness, a tenderness of treatment to the conquered cavalier, which presents a striking contrast to the treatment accorded even the dead by re-enthroned royalty. Cromwell's governmental policy, viewed as a whole, is in no sense open to the charge of cruelty.

But "Cromwell betrayed the cause of liberty." This, if true, expunges the man's name from the roll of patriotism. A traitor! thing to be despised! What are the facts? On what grounds do the charges rest? He became Protector. The war was waged for liberty. Puritanism meant equality. A commonwealth shone in glory before their eyes. The ideal government was now to be inaugurated. Vane, Harrison, Haselrig, dreamed their daydream of democracy. They shut eyes and ears. They were oblivious to the tumultuous seas surging about them. Cromwell knew his country and his time. He held his finger on the nation's pulse. He both heard and saw. He comprehended that the Long Parliament, which had in its life accomplished an epoch-making work, had now lived too long. It was becoming senile. The Commonwealth was speeding to destruction. Anarchy lay but a stone's cast ahead. Clear-visioned Cromwell comprehended this. Than he, no stronger believer in human equality lived. He would have England rule itself without the interposition of army or general; but it was not capable for so herculean a labor. He chose to rule, rather than see the thing for which his army and himself had fought fall into ruin.

England was not ready for self-government. It was not yet grown to man's estate. More than a century must pass before Puritanism would grow so great. Confessedly a nation must have assumed the *toga virilis* before it can be self-controlling. France was incapable of self-government in 1789. The list of victims for the guillotine had not been half so long under a monarchy. It is a grave question whether to this hour the French people are qualified for this duty. The South American republics afford a melancholy spectacle and a suggestive lesson; while Mexico is a republic only in name. Cromwell waited with all patience till he saw whither England was drifting. He knew the brave craft would break to splinters on the rocks. The result subsequent to his death justified his views, and vindicated his motive. It was not a question of Commonwealth or Cromwell; it was a question of Cromwell or Charles II. Cromwell, the great, the heroic, the true; or Charles, the insignificant, the cowardly, the false—which shall rule? Dare any man halt between these extremes? This was the status of national affairs which called forth the resolution and insight of the Puritan statesman. His Protectorate, so far from being a betrayal of liberty, was liberty's preservation.

Having considered the negative phases of this man's character, look at the positive. Cromwell must be studied as soldier, orator, statesman, and man.

And it is as a soldier the world knows him best. That martial figure rivets the world's gaze. He was the soldier pre-eminent of the

Revolutionary period. He rose to be general of all the army by force of achievement and by right of qualification. He was himself. He alone could cope with fiery Rupert. He alone could organize a body of soldiery, whose fame should be as lasting as the world. There was in him the genius of originality and organization. He worked silently and persistently; and from that labor comes the Ironsides, a body of citizen-soldiers, Christians, buckling on the arms of temporal warfare—an organization where rank of mind was superior to rank of blood, a place where men might rise by courage and capacity, an embryonic military republic. This was the new model—praying soldier! Unique creation! Antony, Cæsar, Frederick the Great, were not more original in the cast of their military genius than he. The formation of his army showed his discernment. An army once created, his plan of battle was to drive like a tornado at the enemy's center. He was no Fabius. The peculiarity of the Puritan character was visible in his military tactics. Massive directness, that was all—that was enough. Napoleon was to the end an artillery officer. That stamped all his military operations. Cromwell was to the end a cavalry officer. He fought to win; he fought and won. His was no half-hearted battle; but he bared the blade to smite with all the strength that slumbered in his arm. What Tennyson sings of Wellington, might well be sung of Cromwell. He knew no defeat. His name is a synonym of victory. As a general, he is a pride to England, a glory to the world.

Cromwell as orator! This seems a touch of irony, or at best of acid humor. But he was orator. He had no art of Burke or Fox. He was no Chatham, no Pitt. He had no grace of person, nor fascination of speech. But men heard him. He spoke only when his heart was full. He resorted to speech solely when his silence oppressed him like a nightmare. It was the thought he wished expressed that drove him to speech. His periods were not those of Edward Everett. There was turgidity of style which hints of striving to put much thought within the limits of contracted utterance. He was warrior even in his orations. His vocabulary is Anglo-Saxon. It is often forceful as a battle charge. He did not know circumlocution. In speech, as in battle, he drove at the center. The shortest method to express the thought was the line of advance.

Some of his battle bulletins seem to me as expressive as words could make them. I think no man could hear Cromwell speak and be uncertain as to his meaning. His metaphors are mixed, his sentences ill-balanced; but ambiguity was not among his literary faults. There is, in his addresses as handed down to us, something so stalwart, rugged, soldier-like, that I, for one, can not escape their charm. I am well aware to speak of Cromwell as orator is new, but venture to hope there is more than audacity in the claim.

Cromwell was a statesman. This is high honor to claim for any man. Statesmanship is the ability to discover the trend of events, and to shape the course of national affairs in harmony therewith. Politicians are many, statesmen few. They do not often arise. Mark the procession of legislators and premiers of any nation. Note them with care. See them with vision unobscured by the mists of contemporaneous praise and blame; and the conclusion will be forced upon us, however unsavory it may prove, that the statesmen in any nation's life are lamentably few. Soldier, Cromwell was. The justice of this appellation no one denies; but the qualities of generalship and statesmanship are not often co-existent. A man may be able to mass battalions and execute maneuvers, and be wholly incapable of mastering even the rudiments of statecraft. Illustrations of the truth of this statement multiply in our thought. That Wellington, as a general, was great, let Waterloo declare; but that as a statesman he was below mediocrity, his premiership attests. To the rule as enunciated there are noticeable exceptions; but all such imply a plethora of genius. If Cromwell was statesman as well as general, manifestly he belongs to that illustrious minority who are to be ranked as men of superlative powers.

It is common to say he was no statesman. Eminent authorities are sponsors for this statement. But if statesmanship implies farsighted discernment and ability to achieve success, surely he was a statesman. Cromwell believed in, and unflinchingly advocated, religious toleration. In this the man was a century and more in advance of his times. He brought about the union of England, Ireland, and Scotland. He befriended the American Colonies—a thing no other English king had done. He disfranchised rotten boroughs—a task requiring for its accomplishment the advocacy and diplomacy of leading statesmen of our century. He created the English navy. He attempted to reform the criminal law. He so championed the cause of Protestantism that he brought the Duke of Savoy to a humiliating cessation from persecution. His call assembled the much ridiculed "Barebones Parliament," concerning which it is only just to make two remarks: It was in a high sense a representative body; and did in its enactments forecast many of the most important acts of subsequent English legislation. Cromwell attempted a reform of the Court of Chancery, and succeeded beyond belief. He it was who patronized learned institutions, and first insisted that young men should be trained for the public service in the universities.

These particularizations will suffice to justify the assertion, "Cromwell was a statesman." Many a man has been ranked with statesmen who accomplished not a tithe as much as he. His acts bear the insignia of statesmanship. True it is that many of Cromwell's ventures were not successful. His navies came back defeated; his hopes were unfulfilled. But in his vast schemes it was as in a battle with long battle front. In some places the forces are driven back, in others they charge victoriously onward; and the army as a whole advances with victory burning on its banners. Cromwell's plans, in part frustrated, in part successful, did in their entirety end in success. When his position is considered, and the odds against which he waged a sleepless war are numbered, it is not extravagant to affirm that no English-born king has shown himself so astute a statesman as the Puritan general, Oliver Cromwell.

But far above the what a man achieves is the what he is. Manhood is nobler than genius. No achievement, however brilliant, can compensate for the lack of manliness. The what I am is the superior of what I do. Puritanism emphasized the dignity of man. Such character as that movement produced, England had not seen for centuries. It has too frequently been the case that great intellectual power has been characterized by correspondingly great turpitude. Genius gives license for lust. With Cromwell it was not so. He was pure. His life was clean. Henry VIII was a libertine; Charles I, a liar; Charles II, a second Domitian for lascivious revels.

Cromwell, in striking antithesis, was true to home. He honored his mother. He loved his wife. Their relations were the tenderest. He loved his children. His son, slain in battle, was never absent from his father's loving thought. His daughter dying, the great heart of the soldier broke. About the man was a noble dignity. He had no little lordliness, no assumed superiority which marks the over-elevation of a little soul. He rose not above his place, but to it. He possessed the dignified demeanor of a man "to the manner born." His comportment was such as brought no discredit to the great nation whose head he was. With him, Whitehall was the court of a Christian king. With his successor, it was a home of royal prostitution. Could contrast be more marked? As a man, simple, humble, not intoxicated by his supreme elevation, but brave, pure, tender—he held to God as his soul's Sovereign. The man Cromwell is of colossal mold, fit companion for Cromwell orator, soldier, statesman.

We judge men by what they achieve. Their works do magnify them. The poet's poem is his exaltation, and the painter becomes a name because his canvas glows with hues and forms of imperishable loveliness. This man should be judged by like standard. He was general and ruler. He was great at home and abroad. He commanded the admiration of contemporaries. He made his government to be respected, feared. He gave England imperishable renown. Assuredly, if this man be judged by what he did achieve, he must be ranked, as says Goldwin Smith, "among the chiefest of the sons of men."

Cromwell, the great Protector, lies dying. A storm, fierce, wild, terrible, rages. The general has come into his last battle. He will gird on sword no more. This is his last charge. It is September 3d, anniversary of victory at Dunbar and Worcester. From those conflicts he came forth unscathed. From this he will be carried to his grave. He prays. England prays. The storm exalts itself like a triumphant troop. Illustrious hour in which a great soul may pass "to where, beyond these voices, there is peace." The battle is ended. The hitherto invulnerable chief is slain. Cromwell lies dead.

In Westminster Abbey there is a place for Mary, who lost Calais, and stained her hands with martyr's blood; but for Oliver Cromwell, no place. He sounded his guns on every shore. He lost no principality. He shed no martyr's blood. He championed freedom of conscience. He compelled respect for Anglo-Saxondom. He made England illustrious as the dawn. But for him is no place in the mausoleum where English honor sleeps.

In Westminster Abbey there is a place for Charles II, who made the English court a brothel, who sold Dunkirk to England's most inveterate foe for money to squander on harlots—for him a place in Westminster! But for him who protected the lowliest citizen against the world, who made the Pope to do his bidding, who won Dunkirk with his soldier's hand—for Oliver Cromwell, there is no place in Westminster Abbey. Yet let this stand as an illustrious propriety. No cathedral shall hold him. He belongs to all the world. His fame is the common inheritance of the race.

William the Great of England

The Puritan revolution had come and gone. If its appearance had been sudden and mysterious, its disappearnce was no less so. It had come unheralded like a new knight into the tournament. It had dashed into the tourney with the swiftness of the wind, but had vanished like Lancelot when he fled into the silence of an unknown place to heal him or to die. The rapidity of either transition is the historical wonder of the seventeenth century.

When we attempt the enumeration of the foes with which liberty must always battle, the surprise is, not that she does so little or so tardily, but that she achieves at all. Her foes are legion. The lust of power leaps like a rider into the saddle whenever the slightest opportunity offers. But when liberty has come, formed and fortified her camp, raised her standard, numbered her adherents, formulated her policy, written her constitution in blood, then the enigma is how, in the brief passing of a lustrum or a decade, the very vestiges of her achievements seemed washed away. That the tide, with the whole ocean swelling in its wake, can erase the rude scrawl of the child's name from the sand, is no surprise; but that when the name of liberty has been graven on the rocks with graver's tool, keen enough to carve its way through troops marshaled by kings—that such should be washed out by the impulse of the passing storm is a mystery the mind can never penetrate.

Liberty came. The halo of a youth eternal binds her brow; the strength of centuries of slumbering powers seems gathered in her arm. Armies which have slumbered during a decade of centuries, awake, stirred by the resurrection power of freedom's voice. We thought to see a growing glory. We inferred a perpetual regnancy of such benignant principles. We fell asleep for but an hour, when lo! the face of history has changed. The insignia of subjugation glittered on citizen and soldier, knight and lord. Liberty seems destined to an eternal sequestration. No man knows her grave, nor marked her burial; but all believe her dead. If some man of supreme faith still turns his inspired face toward the future, his fellows mark him a madman and a fool.

Such, in brief, is the survey of the train of events following the enthronement of human brotherhood in the Puritan dominancy. A Cromwell's death, a palsied power, a Richard's abdication, an impending military anarchy or despotism—and Albemarle brought home a banished prince amidst pomp and rejoicing, which had been a royal welcome to a king returning victor from the wars. A dissolute prince has come with bodyguard of harlots, and such welcome as Rome gave Pompey is accorded him. A solecism this, before which apology sits dumb. When had England seen so servile a Parliament as that which knelt, a craven, at the throne of Charles II? His nod was law. They watched his gesture as musicians the baton stroke of their master-spirit. They forecast his wish. They seemed intent on this, that he should heap contumely upon them. Their servility sat upon them like delirium. The king was false to every promise. Obligation of king to subject he thought a figment, and laughed down. Men who had suffered loss of property and blood for the loyalty they had shown Charles Stuart's failing fortunes were neither thought upon nor mentioned. That they had served him must be its own reward. And he, while men thought him a careless, roystering symbol of kingship, was forging fetters for liberty's limbs. And still men saw the shame he brought, the monster vices which were his daily bread, the selling of national honor for pocket pence to squander on courtesans—saw, nor lifted voice. They saw the glory which Cromwell bought by splendid achievement, pale to gray and gloom; and England became a jest to all Europe! And still they bowed at their Domitian's throne. To affirm, under such inculcation as these facts afford, that liberty was dead seems but a superfluity. It would rather appear she had never lived.

If we may reason from their conduct, the Stuarts accounted ingratitude a virtue. Clarendon, who supplied the statesmanship for the reign of Charles II, as Strafford had done for that of Charles I, discovered that royalty had no remembrance of service loyally and ably performed. If Charles I let Strafford perish on the block despite the royal promise to save him at every hazard, Charles II, despite the long years of his secretary's faithfulness in times of exile, despite every incentive to a gratitude that should have known neither metes nor bounds, drove him from his royal presence. If the king, dying, whispered, "Remember poor Nell," it is but candor to remark that mistresses were the only persons who could boast his substantial regard. Men, court, and England itself, must be sold in the shambles to gratify the passions of this libidinous lord.

But Charles is dead. James II ascends the throne. His brother was a jester till he died. This man is bigoted, morose, and sullen as winter. Yet with his failings he is superior to Charles by unnumbered gradations. Those who bore the shame of the reign of Charles II should not have murmured at the tyranny of James. Charles masked his malice with a smile; James moved toward his destined end with knit brows. This it was that slew him. If ever there was a desert in the history of liberty, it was in the epoch succeeding the protectorate of mighty Cromwell, and extending to the abdication of James II. Yet even that desert was to bloom with beauty; and liberty was only sleeping, and not dead. And this was the hour which was to witness the coming of William, the greatest English king after Cromwell.

Of the four Williams named in the list of English kings, two were foreigners. The men of strength were foreign born. William Rufus and William IV added names to the list of kings, but have made history no richer because they reigned. But of the first and third William, history may well be voluble. They differed in nationality, time, character. One was a Norman, and founded the British Empire; the other was Dutch, and refounded, on a nobler plan, the government which had fallen so low men thought it could no more arise. They lived six centuries apart.

William I was cruel. He seemed to revivify the spirit of Attila and Alaric. He was iron-handed, and, in his bursts of passion, fierce even to frenzy. Self-restraint he did not so much as know by name. He embodied the strength and weakness of Feudalism. A continental feudal lord, he raised himself to be an island king. Atilla the Hun was not more ferocious; and no inroad of buccaneers, Saxon or Danish, was ever more terrible than his conquest. His caress was cruel. His smile had no sunlight in it. He peopled England with desolation. He banished the Saxon from camp and palace, and thought he had made a perpetual banishment. William I was ruthlessness enthroned. But historians allow the man was no mediocre. In a fierce age he outmatched its fierceness; but there was in him a genius for control. He curbed his fierce barons. His vengeance appalled them. Love he did not expect, and cared not for. Obedience he demanded and enforced with terrible severities. His shaggy brows beetled over eyes that saw. Statesmanship was in him. He was the greatest statesman of his century.

Six stormy centuries pass. Norman, Plantagenet, Lancaster, York, Tudor, Stuart, each has his day. Feudalism lives to totter in decrepitude; and the last feudal baron, king-making Warwick, closes the gate that shuts mediæval England out for evermore. There is struggle for liberty at Runnymede, at Naseby, in Star-chamber, in Parliament. Tower Hill is crimson with patriot's blood. We seem to be spectators of the horrors of an opium-eater's dream. Another king ascends the throne. His mien betrays his kingliness. The third William is the antithesis of the first. His is the spirit of modern Europe. His whole life is an apocalypse of self-control. He is a warrior, but not a marauder and assassin calling himself a king. He humbles the pride of the French sovereign, when that monarch had prevailed in the face of all Europe. By his accession the English struggle for constitutional liberty was terminated triumphantly; and it thus happens that William is a man important, not only for himself, but also for the drama in whose closing scene he acted.

He is a man who challenges remembrance, both for what he was and what he did. But if to this there be added an illustrious field for the display of ability, and momentous events which missed being tragic because he was present, then clearly a more absorbing interest attaches to him. He becomes the more important, and must be interrogated if we are to comprehend one of the most unique and important epochs of modern history.

William III was a native of the United Netherlands. Born in 1650, died in 1702, his eventful life spanned an eventful half-century. He belonged to a race distinguished alike for industry and love of liberty. The Dutch had wrested the land they inhabited from the ocean. In Cæsar's time, Holland was a series of marshes verging on the Northern seas. By a matchless industry, that uninhabited and uninhabitable waste had become the most fertile tract in Europe. This land became the refuge for the persecuted Puritans of England; and from its shores, Puritan America set sail. The Dutch had become a race of seafaring merchantmen, whose vessels entered every harbor of the earth. They planted colonies in the New World, and founded as their capital that city which has become the metropolis of modern America. It was fitting that a people so distinguished for industry should become renowned in the annals of liberty, and so it was. The Dutch set the English an example in resisting kingly tyranny. The encroachments of the bigoted, imperious Philip spurred them into rebellion. The Inquisition, with its unimagined horrors, goaded the people to veritable frenzy; and some of the most noble records of human heroism are to be found in the battles and sieges of this remarkable people. Under the leadership of William the Silent, a man of splendid genius, of catholicity of spirit rarely equaled, and of a breadth of view surpassed only by breadth of patriotism,—under the leadership of such a man the Netherlands became free.

William III was scion of a noble house,

and the inheritor of qualities which made William the Silent a figure fit for the pantheon of the world. In frame, he was slender and feeble. The citadel of his life was beset by asthma and consumption. His life was a conquest of an indomitable will over seemingly impossible odds. His forehead was capacious, his cheek pale, his expression sullen, his manner incongenial. He was taciturn, and seldom smiled. He repelled men, rather than attracted them. Only in time of battle did his manners become gracious, his smile sunny, and his mien truly lordly. In feebleness of frame, he reminds us of Torstenson, the illustrious successor of Gustavus Adolphus. In generalship, he was a second William the Silent. In statescraft, he stands, as Macaulay affirms, "the peer of Richelieu."

William III was the great-grandson of William the Silent, and posthumous son of William II, Prince of Orange, "and was," as Kitchen affirms, "destined to be the most distinguished man of his race." That such was to be his elevation, there was nothing to forecast. At his birth the sun of the House of Orange seemed set. "Father William" had been slain by a hired assassin of Phillip II.

Prince Maurice, as a brilliant soldier, had continued the heroic enterprise for freedom, to which his father had dedicated his fortune and his life. On his death, in 1625, Frederick Henry, his brother, seized the spear which had fallen from Maurice's dying grasp, and wielded it right royally for two and twenty years. In 1648 the Netherlands were recognized as free. They were Spanish dependencies no more.

The House of Orange had liberated the the Lowlands. Such service, it would appear, merited recognition and reward; but William II, son of Frederick, was supremely ambitious, and, it is to be feared, supremely selfish. His grandfather had been the servant of his country; the grandson estimated the country his body-servant, to do his bidding. Such ambition "o'erleaped itself." At his death the States General abolished the stadtholdership. The government became an aristocratic republic, with virtual kingly power in the hands of the Grand Pensionary, John DeWitt; and William of Orange grew up the acknowledged head of a semi-monarchical party, at once hated, watched, and feared. His words, looks, and gestures were recorded. Suspicion guarded him on every side. He had been hedged with enemies from his childhood. Hence, says Protherou, "William learned caution, reserve, insight into character, and the art of biding his time." He had come to guard his thoughts as soldiers do the palace of the king. Any but a prophet would have said the glory of the House of Orange had departed. The youth of Frederick the Great gave indefinitely more promise than that of William; and men did not, could not know that this, the last of an illustrious house, was to become the chief personality of contemporaneous Europe.

These infelicitous surroundings afford some clue to the character of Orange. They do not account for it. Environment never can account for either character or conduct. At best it casts but a feeble light. It is never more than an adjunct. But doubtless those traits of the prince which made him so unpopular as an English sovereign had thus been burned the deeper into his soul.

Deterrents to popularity were elemental in his career as general and statesman. His face never betrayed him. He hid behind it as behind a mask. Though joy laughed in his heart, his face was sunless, his eyes lusterless.

Praise or blame, victory or defeat, he met with visage unperturbed. Men looked in vain to read the secrets he hid in his capacious mind. Diplomats could get no word which should betray the plans he was maturing for the accomplishment of that end to which he had dedicated every power of his soul—that end the humiliation of Louis XIV and the enfranchisement of Europe. And when the year 1672 came, and with it the battalions of Louis's unequaled soldiers to wash like a storm-sea over the Netherlands, William, the lad of twenty-two, was in truth a man of mature intellect and vigor, fit to cope with the greatest sovereign of Europe.

Since the Dutch had, in 1667, become a party to the Triple Alliance, Louis had determined to annihilate Holland. At that time he was the statesman pre-eminent of all Christendom. With him diplomacy took shape as an art in government, and with it he conquered in the cabinets of kings. His diplomacy had served to detach every ally from Holland, and leave it as friendless as the beggar shivering at the gate. Thus, alone and armyless, the republic must meet upon the field of blood the best-trained soldiers of the century. The provinces were panic-stricken. That was William's hour. He rose to meet the storm. He met it as the sailor the tempest, with courage like to joy. He roused his provinces to resistance. He gave his revenues and private fortune to the State, to be used in defense. He took the lead of its armies. He stood in the swirl of battle undisturbed, even joyful. He opened the sluices and flooded vast tracts, as William the Silent had done before him. He was heroism at its best. He formed confederations against France. He won no battle; but such was his genius for turning defeat into triumph that Turenne and Condé, though always victors, were always defeated. Condé retired, Turenne died; but William lived to celebrate, in 1678, the treaty of Nimeguen and the independence of Holland. Small wonder that his countrymen loved him with an affection near to adoration. The ten years which had succeeded this triumphant peace were, on William's part, an era of diplomacy. He headed the coalition of Europe. A country with scant ten thousand square miles of territory dominates in the councils of emperors; so does genius master.

Had the stadtholder never become a king,

had his base of action never been enlarged from a province to a kingdom, William III would have ranked among the great men of Modern Europe. It was not place made him great. When he became king of England, it was he who honored England, not England which honored him.

From the time of his marriage with Mary, daughter of the Duke of York, William had turned the attention of his astute intellect to England and English politics. He cast covetous eyes upon the throne, because as the sovereign of one of the great powers of Europe he could more effectually head the coalitions against the arch enemy of continental powers, the king of France. It is safe to assume that never in waking hours did the prince forget that king whose life was spent in self-adulation and in plans for the aggrandizement of himself and Catholicism. William was the acknowledged head of Protestant Europe. If he cared for England's crown, for such common ambition as the many know, that desire is not apparent. With him the kingship of England was a means, and not, as with others, an end.

The haughtiness of Louis becomes insupportable. He domineers over Europe. He revokes the Edict of Nantes. James, with that folly characteristic of the Stuarts, goads his people into anger he can not allay. William is invited to England to save English liberties. He does not haste. He feels the pulse of England, till he knows the hour has come. Then he gathers his troops, sets sail for Torbay, lands on the island kingdom, and heads his columns toward London. The die is cast. The glorious revolution hastens to accomplishment.

The travesty and the pathos of the revolution of 1688 lies in this, that patriotism played so insignificant a part. Love of freedom was not so much a factor as the hatred for the saturnine James. Anomalous as the statement is, love of liberty was inferior to love of perjury. That so benignant a revolution should have such paternity seems impossible, but is only melancholy truth. Marlborough, who owed all to his master, James, was foremost in conspiring against him, hoping in change of masters to increase gains. His spirit was the spirit of his compeers. Besides Somers, Nottingham, and possibly Montague, it is hard to name an English statesman of the reign of William III who was a man of incorruptible honor.

All this goes to show the influence of a reign like that of Charles II. Charles died, but the blight of his reign survived him. Dishonor was to him instead of honor; and that statesmen trained in such a school should have been traitors for a coronet is not hard to believe. When had political virtue been so low? The virtue of those men who championed the Puritan revolution was so unimpeachable, and their character so clean, that their memory is like precious odors. They had the flavor of divine moralities. They entertained elevated conceptions of honor. But with the return of the Stuarts there was a reinstatement of depraved political codes. Those who hoped to receive honors from the king's munificence, must bring their purchase-money in their hands. All England was an object of barter. The king received bribes from France; he must also receive bribes from England. Like lord, like liege. The antecedents of the revolution of 1688, England may well hope to forget: the result of it she may well pray to hold in everlasting remembrance. Corrupt governments are always a curse to both present and future. The vitiated morals of this period make solemn comment on the curse of corrupt kings.

But history is one. Unpropitious to liberty as the times seemed, they were not more so than those which antedate the rise of the Dutch Republic. He who reads the records of that era to a certain point will come to question whether Holland had any man save one, and whether liberty were not a lost art. The Netherlands suffered the Inquisition to do its worst. Its sons wore the shackles of a galling servitude, and refused to break them. Execrable cruelties seemed powerless to change them from cowards into men. That Orange could have believed in them through it all is one of the miracles of human faith. Egmont and Horn were purchased with a smile. Many another exchanged his honor as a thing of barter. Yet out of such sterile soil had risen a gigantic growth. And the Batavian Republic stood the foremost republic in Europe and in the world.

So, in the light of history, England's cause was not altogether hopeless. The very perfidy, the dishonor, the shameless treason of men highest in the counsels of the king, were made under God the ministers of constitutional liberty.

Four and a half centuries of struggle for constitutional liberty were marshaling squadrons for their last onset. This was, as we now know, a solemn and majestic moment. In the last charge is always something fathomless in tragic interest. The pathos of that final charge of Napoleon's life-guard is fit to make men weep. All life flung into one awful hour is a spectacle before which silence is the only fitting speech. The Anglo-Saxon is now to make one more massive onset. It is the Marathon of king or constitution. From Runnymede and John to Whitehall and James, the march has been one long struggle between absolutism and constitutional rights. The shout and tumult of battle have been incessant. It was in such a scene that William III was called upon to be the kingly actor.

Two things are requisite that a drama may be sublime,—noble stage and noble actor. These two elements are met this hour. The destinies of liberty, for which Puritans have been glad to die, were marching to triumph or death. The battle-piece is sublime; and

Orange is a fit figure to hold his place on such a scene. For such an hour he was the man of destiny. He it was who made victory achievable. His whole life seemed preparation for this exigency of liberty. His was that tutoring of adversity which makes men meet for any hazard. He had been schooled

> "To throw away the dearest thing he owned,
> As 't were a careless trifle."

And at the end he might have said with Richard III,

> "And I have set my life upon a cast,
> And I will stand the hazard of the die."

Subtraction is sometimes an easy and lucid method of finding the value of a given quantity. Heat eliminated, the world, which is so fair, would become a barren ice-waste, flowerless as the region of the pole. Moisture subtracted, the planet would wheel to every sunrise one hot Sahara, with no oasis to offer fountain and rest and cooling shade. The earth would be a fevered giant, for whose delirium no febrifuge could avail. Use this method in determining the value of William of Orange as a factor in that revolution which gave to England a new meridian. Suppose he had not been.

What could England have done? Whither could it have looked for aid? Where was there a man in Europe to whose hands Parliament would have felt safe in intrusting the scepter?

Is it not clear that but for William that gracious revolution had not been for a century or centuries? It appears plain that, in any conservative estimate, to William, England must be debtor for the clear gain of at least a hundred years of constitutional government. Small wonder then that a test of fealty to the progressive party in English politics has been loyalty to the memory of their great deliverer, William of Orange. His presence and coming simplified the problem, and rendered a solution possible. In this light, his value to Anglo-Saxondom and the world is impossible to overestimate.

The battles for liberty have been won by scant populations. The few sowed, the many reap. The population of the Netherlands, in the era of the struggle for freedom from Spanish possessions, numbered three millions. That of America at the time of its Revolution was the same. The census of England at the time of the Revolution was five millions. It seems beyond belief that this supreme triumph for constitutionality was won by populations only a trifle larger than that of London of the present; but so it was. The few are benefactors, the many beneficiaries.

The succession of events following William's landing and preceding his coronation, is briefly rehearsed. James desires to treat. William astutely accedes to the request. The king takes advice from his timorous heart, and flees; is captured and returned, to the chagrin of the prince; escapes again; destroys the writs of convocation, disbands the army, throws the great seal into the Thames, takes ship with wife and babe for France; and,—*finis* to the Stuarts. It is fit termination of Stuart sovereignty; and for such self-exile there can be no return.

In the light of succeeding events, England can have no more celebrated anniversary than November 5th, the date of William's landing. How stupendous the undertaking on which he entered, no one but himself comprehended. His solemn farewell to the States of Holland is full of pathos. He says he is leaving them "perhaps not to return." Should he fall in defense of the reformed religion and the independence of Europe, he commends his beloved wife to their care. These utterances affirm how well the prince knew the gravity of the undertaking on which he was now embarked. During the reign of Charles II, England had been a dependency of the French crown. James had pledged himself to continue this relation. Add to this the bigotry of James and the complete surrender of his narrow nature to Catholicism, and the rock on which the cause of Protestantism was drifting looms terribly through the fog.

Such men as Phillip II, Louis XIV, and James II, open a strange chapter to students of psychology. These men were barren in all that affection characteristic of great souls. They were as selfish as the desert, which ingulfs all streams, but gives back no fountain. Yet the love these men gave Rome was as extravagant and absolute as the donors were bigoted and malignant. William did not battle with shadows. He did not misconstrue the writing on the wall. The union of Catholic England and Catholic France with a single ruler for the two, and he such a man as Louis XIV, meant the destruction of liberty and Protestantism so far as this was a possibility of human machination. Three years before, the revocation of the Edict of Nantes had shown to an astonished Europe the length to which the bigotry of the French sovereign would drive him. These facts loomed ominously before the eyes of Prince William, and impelled him to venture all, that he might save all.

This is a legitimate interpretation of the Declaration of Rights. It has no insular meaning. If it meant much to the island kingdom, it meant scarcely less to the continental kingdoms. Its stipulations, sown to the tides of air and sea, and borne to every continent, are therefore familiar to the world. In a word, the "Declaration" means the supremacy of the people. The king becomes elective, and appears the creation of Parliament, not Parliament the creation of the king. This was fit climax of Magna Charta; and thus the English Constitution, that great, unwritten document, was completed. On February 13, 1689, at Whitehall, William and Mary became joint sovereigns under such limitations. England became, in fact as well as in legal fiction, a constitutional monarchy; and the Glorious Revolution was consummated. No bloody assize comes with William's reign. That belongs to the execrable atrocities of Jeffreys and of James. William's motto, "I will maintain," was supplemented by, "the liberties of England and the Protestant religion." Such was his splendid purpose; such his still more splendid achievement.

The recording these events which made William king is a task easy of accomplishment; but the magnitude of the undertaking was sufficient to have appalled a soul less great. Macaulay says: "One capacious and powerful mind alone took all the difficulties into view, and determined to surmount them all," and "the whole history of ancient and modern times records no such triumph of statesmanship." High tribute this; but the lapse of time demands no revision of statement. But the task on which the king entered was, if possible, as arduous as the one just completed. The declaration, when once in the nation's blood and circulating in its veins, was to introduce the most memorable changes which have occurred in the whole history of England.

William was born to be king. The qualities of mind and heart which justify kingship he possessed in an eminent degree. Hallam says: "The desire of rule in William III was as magnanimous and public-spirited as ambition can ever be in human bosom." Such a man may be trusted with supreme powers. Had he been an autocrat the thirteen years of his sovereignty would doubtless have brought such humiliation to France as Crecy or Malplaquet wrought. With powers like Napoleon, he had ground Louis into powder. But in his plan he was often like a boat locked in harbor by adverse winds. Time and tide are propitious, but the bark can not slip from the mooring. England could not see through William's eyes. That required his genius. He must first master Parliament, then the councils of Europe. The conflict was a bitter one. Small wonder that sometimes he cried out like a wounded man, and would have resigned the sovereignty, and retired to Holland.

Yet it was better that one king, attempered for benignant rule, be hampered unduly than other kings of common sort should reign without control. The historian above quoted avers that "William was too great for his time," and "the last sovereign of this country whose understanding and energy of character have been distinguished." For that reason the Declaration of Rights must prevail. English liberties must be maintained. In this view the very humiliation of so great a king was a triumph of the Revolution, whose master spirit he was.

William saw that continued war with France was the price England must pay for its freedom. That is the key to his diplomacy and sleepless activity. Louis sheltered the dethroned king, and championed his cause with money, arms, diplomatic agents. The war of 1689 was the solitary thing which saved the independence of England. The British people had moments of vision; but the glory of events blinded them. But the king saw on. William's whole life was one long campaign against France, of which his life as king was only a part. He formed the Grand Alliance, and was its soul. No other could animate so huge a thing. Sublime powers are requisite to breathe life into a great coalition. He spent part of each year on the Continent leading the armies of Europe against their common foe. He routed Louis and James at the battle of the Boyne. That victory assured his throne. He conquered at Namur; but defeat on the battle-field was his lot more often than triumph. His victories came when the battle was ended. France won the fight: William carried off the spoils; and in 1697 the peace of Ryswick vindicated the statesmanship of William, when, says Green, "for the first time since Richelieu's day, France consented to a disadvantageous peace; in spite of failures and defeats in the field William's policy had won."

The difficulties with which the king coped were legion. A new power given the people made them captious. The king, though the savior of England's liberties, was goaded almost to madness by being trusted less than the Stuarts. This, as has been shown, was a necessity of the Revolution, but none the less harassing to a proud spirit for that reason. He was beleaguered by traitors. Members of his cabinet were plotting for the return of James. As in the case of his famous ancestor, a price was put upon his head. James offered a coronet to the assassin of the king. The treasury was depleted by the iniquitous reigns of Charles and James. The coin was debased. Continental wars were a source of expense till then unknown. Taxes were in consequence high, and dissatisfaction prevalent. The Tories were avowed Jacobites, and as soon as impending fear fell from them by the coronation of William, leisure and opportunity were afforded for every species of iniquitous practice which infected their blood. No English king besides Cromwell was so beset by foes, and no king except Cromwell was so great.

In William's time England was a cesspool of political vices. Honor was a word whose significance was lost. To know the extent of the perfidy of this era, let a man read Dalrymple, Macaulay, and the Shrewsbury correspondence. A querulous Parliament, the most stupendous war England had known to that hour, plans which were too large for popular comprehension,—all these made the burdens of the king almost insupportably weighty. Meantime he suffered, but England grew great. The spell of his genius touched even it at the last.

Before proceeding to the examination of the remarkable constitutional changes which belong to the reign of King William, it is well to pause for a moment to note those qualities of mind and heart in the king, which, aside from his genius, adapted him for leadership in the regeneration of a kingdom. These,

I take it, are five in number,—his ability to grasp principles, his humaneness, his freedom from bigotry, his self-forgetfulness, and his courage. These qualities go far toward making an ideal king. The first implies statesmanship, which was displayed on all occasions, and led to the adoption of Sunderland's policy for organizing the ministry from the party in power,—one of the most sagacious expedients ever resorted to in government.

William's humaneness was of incalculable worth in England. The people were spendthrifts of blood. Tower Hill was a place easy of access; English mobs had been proverbially ferocious. The terrible penal code in vogue more than a hundred years later leaves no need for further proof of the truth of the statement. William was granite here. No bloodshed must be tolerated on his enthronement. He was as humane as Cromwell in his administration. The result was what we might anticipate. The value of such precedent was priceless. It taught England that political stability could be secured without constant appeal to a headsman's ax and gibbet. His act of amnesty was a service to mankind in the spirit it exhibited. In this sketch there is no desire to obscure any facts in the life of King William. All will bear inspection. Three acts may be adduced, which, more than any others, would seem to smirch his name. The mob massacre of the De Witts, the attack on Mons subsequent to the treaty of peace, and the massacre of Glencoe. It may be said that the most hostile and virulent criticism has not been able, in any proper sense, to connect William with these. Whether he was culpable or not, we do not know. He may not have risen enough above the spirit of his age to have been free from taint; but it is safe to allege that the tenor of his life, the humanity of his behavior, do not favor the theory of his guilt in these cases. Let a man's history answer for his conduct, and the motives which prompt it when that conduct is uncertain. This is a just and magnanimous rule.

Self-forgetfulness had ample room for exercising itself in his case. Had he been other than he was, he could have deluged his realm with blood. He chose to pass by ingratitude, even treason. He won Shrewsbury, and disarmed Marlborough by seeming unconsciousness of their treason. With him the end to which his life was dedicated was supreme. He was nothing; it was all. In that attitude lie unknown possibilities for good.

The king's freedom from religious bigotry is one of his noblest traits. That is always a safe mark of a manly soul. Hallam says, "He was in all things superior to his subjects;" certainly in none more remarkably than this. History has memory of few more noble utterances than his declaration against religious persecution. In this, too, the mantle of William the Silent seems to have fallen upon him. Under him Dissenters were allowed rights which were inalienably theirs. Such was his catholicity of sentiment that he would have removed the ban from the Catholic as well; and it was one of the charges brought against him by virulent opposition that he connived at popery.

William was courageous. That is a king's trait. He compelled the admiration of the greatest soldiers of Europe by his dauntless courage. As a lad, he led his soldiers, and stood in the midst of battle's tempest. He could in one way, he said, prevent seeing his country conquered, and that was "By dying in the last ditch." Only heroism pronounces such words. His passing into Ireland to vanquish James, when treason was rife in England, Green pronounces one of the bravest deeds of his heroic life.

Those changes in government, some of which are valuable beyond computation, may be mentioned, but not elaborated. Such are: Triennial Parliaments, vote of annual supplies, the Mutiny Act, establishment of the Bank of England and the reform of the debased coin, the national debt and its effect in rendering the revolution stable, change of ministry with change of party, Religious Toleration Act, allowing Scotland its own Church, annual assembly of Parliament, and the right of Parliamentary inquiry. What other period of equal length, or thrice that, can produce such a catalogue of signal gains for posterity? Divine right of kings became an extinct doctrine, the maintenance of a standing army without the consent of Parliament was rendered impossible, the national debt became a defense rather than a danger,—these and more were the fruits of a reign of thirteen years. Beyond controversy, this proved an illustrious reign.

William was an unpopular sovereign. At a two-century remove it is hard to give this credence. He had in the largest sense befriended England. He had rescued her from an infamy unspeakable. He had lifted her from a state of dependency on her most determined foe, and made her the chief government of Europe. Such services as these merit a reward as generous as the service was illustrious. As logic, this reasoning is perfect; as history, it is wide of the truth. England had few more unpopular sovereigns than William. This statement is not flattering to the intelligence of the English people, but is undeniably true. It is not difficult to discover reasons for this unpopularity, a few of which may be assigned.

The king's taciturnity militated against him. The easy suavity of manner characteristic of Charles II and Marlborough he did not possess. His was a great nature, but was not voluble. There were deeps in his heart men knew not of. But to his best beloved he appeared a princely soul apart from his inheritance. Portland knew him, and his wife loved him to the verge of adoration. His voice was harsh, his manner dry and brusque. He had no easy joviality. He was not a figure framed for court society. Easy affability he did not possess. Worth, manliness, courage, and virtue were his; but these, men could not see, and so it is easy to discover that the geniality which had been so marked in the manner of Charles, but was so lacking in that of William, should have brought a contrast to the king's hurt. Men are easily deceived. They do not pierce beneath the thin disguise of externality to discover genuine and unapproachable merit.

Another chief cause of William's unpopularity was his partiality to his own countrymen. He loaded Portland with honors. He gave great estates to those who had been his lifelong friends. There is a sense in which this charge is just. If by undue partiality is meant that he was impolitic, then there can be no controverting facts: it was impolitic. To have dispossessed him of all those friends who had counted life for his sake a worthless thing, would have given him a popularity he did not possess. The Dutch constituents of the king stood, as the politicians supposed, between themselves and preferment. This was a sin they could not pardon. By ingratitude such as the Stuarts had schooled England to expect, William could have crowned himself with ephemeral popularity; but this man was not of the Stuart sort. In that lay his pre-eminent fitness for kingship. He had a heart. He loved his friends. He really supposed that being a king did not disqualify him from being a man, and acting a manly part. He had a memory for those whose life had been to do his service. He was indiscreet sometimes in loading his tried friends with unneeded honors, but such error may easily be forgotten. Would the Stuarts had been given to such weakness and such vice! But if sacrifices for his sake were thought on, the second Charles would hold his hand to be kissed by the men who had risked all and lost all for his sake, and pay for a life of service so devoted as to make succeeding generations marvel, by a "God bless you, my old friend." William was a man both before and after his coronation. Gratitude was a peculiarity of his character. He held to his friends with a tenacity which knew no abatement, even when it threatened the stability of his throne.

There is, too, another fact which must not be forgotten or obscured. The king was among a race of statesmen to whom political virtue was a jest. This melancholy phase of this period has been adverted to, but can not receive too much emphasis. Every man seemed determined to sell his honor's birthright. Members of the king's ministry, the commanders of his fleet and of his army, were traitors to his every interest. Loyalty was a word whose meaning they did not know. The record of the shameless treasons of those times makes modern England blush at the mere remembrance. That a king thus beset, with his halls crowded with traitors, should have leaned as on a staff upon friends whose loyalty was as certain and inalienable as the affections of the lovely woman who loved to be called his wife, is not strange nor blamable. It is rather the wisdom of the profoundest statesman of his times.

William was a foreigner. This was a fruitful source of unpopularity. He was a native of the one country which had contested with England the sovereignty of the seas. The two commercial countries of Europe were now England and Holland. Such rivalry as existed between Genoa and Venice burned hot between the country which gave William birth and the one over which he swayed scepter as king. In ports even at the antipodes the Dutch and English merchantmen were competitors. Englishmen were therefore jealous of any favor shown to their commercial rivals.

William belonged to that nation; and every sign of love for his country or his countrymen seemed to their distempered vision a slight to England and Englishmen. He and those he favored were Hollanders. The first they could forget, the second never.

What England had suffered from the introduction of foreign troops ought, however, to be urged as a slight palliation for this feeling. Even William's government was constantly threatened by the French and Irish army; and during the encroachments of Charles I, with his usual perfidy, he planned deluging his kingdom with Catholic battalions. Since the time of William the Conqueror, the English had tended toward insularity. Their aversion to foreign encroachments had been as bitter as winter. The Church of Rome was detested mainly for this reason. It thus arose naturally, if not wisely, that the foreign troops of William's guard were endured with distrust, and, in 1697, over the manifest protest of the king and in spite of his service, they were compelled to return to Holland. This spirit of rancorous dislike to what was foreign was no insignificant factor in the unpopularity of William. His splendid service, when fresh in memory, in spite of their natural dislike, won him the flitting popularity he possessed.

The English statesmen who gathered about William the king were men of superior abilities. Danby, Shrewsbury, Halifax, Devonshire, Montague, Marlborough, Sunderland, Godolphin, Portland, Somers, were men who, for strength of intellect, grasp of mind, and variety of genius, have not often been paralleled in the annals of England. With a few notable exceptions, they were as prominent for statesmanlike parts as they were lacking in patriotism. Their genius was as brilliant as their honor was tarnished; yet "compared with William," says the judicial Hallam, "the statesmen who surround his throne sink into insignificance." Green calls him "a born statesman." Statescraft seemed his daily bread. His capacity for mastering men, for forming gigantic coalitions, for wringing victory from sore defeat, for bearing up against seas of adversity, for holding himself in imperturbable calm amidst the very tragedies of his career, seems incredible. Viewed from whatever point, his plans were great,—great in moral heroism, great in the courage that can brook delay, great in achieving results which shall endure.

Statesmanship is an appeal from bodily to intellectual force. With it armies are of secondary value; and its introduction is a supplanting of soldier by diplomat. To Louis XI of France men owe a debt difficult to repay, for he it was who shifted the fray from the field of battle to the cabinet. His was a powerful though a depraved intellect. But, though he substituted cunning for force, in it were the roots from which grew that large and beneficent life we name statesmanship. Hitherto France had seemed to have a monopoly of diplomatic skill. William the Silent and Cromwell had been the most illustrious statesmen who had arisen outside of France. Louis XIV had ruled Europe through his crafty diplomacy.

Statesmanship in the sense of manipulating great interstate interests, found no place with Cæsar or Augustus; for Rome was the one nation, and did not treat, but conquered. And so it is safe to affirm that the greatest international statesmen who had lived thus far were Richelieu and William III, and the coronation of William introduced England into the affairs of continental Europe, as it had not been in its long and splendid history. The wars of the Edwards for the possession of French principalities, as well as the insignia of royalty, were mere contests between two kingdoms. There the belligerency ended. At that period diplomacy was a thing little understood. Gigantic coalitions, such as burdened the world with armies, and made Europe the theater of battle, were inaugurated by the enthronement of William III. The coalitions of Henry VIII and Elizabeth were bagatelles compared with what came later. Cromwell made England a word of mighty import; but he dominated in the councils as an august power, whose wrath, when kindled but a little, meant disaster. Cromwell was primarily a soldier; William, primarily a statesman. This marks the difference in their genius. By statesmanship, William made England a proud figure in deciding the destinies of Europe, and there could be no more isolation. The campaigns of Marlborough and Wellington, with all the supremacy they gave, were fruits of William's diplomacy. "An alliance was made" became a phrase introduced into the nomenclature of European statescraft as soon as

William came into power. He organized the greatest combination Europe had seen since the Crusades. That is his genius. He lost battles, but ruled Europe. Not the strength of his armies, but the might of his diplomacy made him the prince omnipotent among the statesmen of his time. His coronation changed England from an insular government to a continental realm. He flung her into the vortex of continental affairs, from which there can be no escape. He made England a force even as he had previously made the Batavian Republic. William's death, we are told, "shook the Grand Alliance" to its very base. The interpretation of all the acts of his diversified career is to be sought in one word—statesmanship.

In recalling scenes among the mountains, one will always linger longer than others, like a lover when the guests are gone. Its sublime solitudes, its rocky summits whitened with unwasting snows, its armies of silent pines that stand and wait as for the general's "Forward," the lake whose chalice seems to hold the blue washed from the sky through centuries,—even so, one thing greets me first, and challenges me last, in thinking of William III, imperial crag among the mountain fastnesses of history. His royal statesmanship captivates my thought, and casts its spell over me as a sunset does.

Yet the choicer characteristics of this man were visible only to the few; and all the splendor of his achievements and the supremacy of his genius find fitting complement in his life, and termination in his death. His love, like his genius, was profound; and at the death of Mary, who had been so beautiful in her affection for him, he raved like a storm at midnight. He died as he had lived—a man. "No weakness or querulousness," says the brilliant historian of his reign, "disgraced the noble close of that noble career." In the midst of paroxysms of pain, he was thoughtful and courteous. He planned for England to the last; and when too weak to take his place upon the throne, he wrote urging the union of England and Scotland. To the end, as all his life, his thought was for others, and not for self. Men knew he prayed, from the fragments of petitions that fell from his lips, as we know in darkness the sea is near by the music of waves upon the rocks. He called for the dearest friend of his life, and when no longer able to speak, took his hand and pressed it fondly to his breast. Thus he died; and above his heart they found a ring of gold and a lock of Mary's hair. So set that sun whose beams have given to England an unsetting day.

The Greater English Elegies

THE elegy springs from the heart as flowers from the grave. It is grief finding a voice. And so long as hearts love and lose, so long will the elegy be native to us as tears. If you shall listen to the voices of the wind at night, you shall seem to hear elegiacs. Nature turns to sobbing with such naturalness as brings her into companionship with hearts that break and voices that find their utterance a sob. Since graves are always freshly made, and lives freshly bereft, the elegy, least of all poetry, can become archaic.

English literature is genius trying all instruments of music. Certain it is that the elegies here characterized have no peers, but stand a sacred and solitary quaternion. They are here mentioned in their chronological order. This apostolic succession runs: Milton, Gray, Shelley, Tennyson; and the productions: Lycidas, Elegy in a Country Churchyard, Adonais, In Memoriam,—and the arch spans two centuries of elegiacs. With one exception, the poems are personal. Gray's elegy is impersonal.

Sorrow usually dissipates when general. We can not commiserate men-kind save in mankind. This personal element is apparent in all grief. Elegies are the soul crying aloud, "Absalom, my son, my son!" and in those rare instances when not special we still seem brooding as at a grave. This mourning dove is mourning for our dead. We reduce to the singular all pluralizations of grief. In Thanatopsis, an elegy in a noble vein, the spirit is individualized in the closing strain:

"So live, that when thy summons comes to join
  The innumerable caravan that moves
To that mysterious realm where each shall take
His chamber in the silent halls of death,
Thou go not like the quarry slave at night,
Scourged to his dungeon, but sustained and
    soothed
By an unfaltering trust, approach thy grave
Like one who wraps the drapery of his couch
About him, and lies down to pleasant dreams."

It is "thy death" to which all this accord of music points. Milton, Shelley, Tennyson, poets, but men none the less, loved friends, and since death came, each lifted up his voice and wept like one of old. Milton's friend, Edward King, died in shipwreck on the Irish

Sea; Shelley's friend, that modern Greek, John Keats, died under the blue of Roman skies, calling, "I feel the violets growing over me." Tennyson's friend, Arthur Hallam, a youth of rare though unfulfilled promise, died and found the health he sought in heaven. These poems are apostrophes, while Gray's is a monologue, as of one who sits alone in the shadow of the yew in calm beside a grave.

Life itself is not more stimulating to fancy than death. Poetry seems native to both estates. Above the gorge of Niagara, in the fringes of a pine wood, all but in hearing of the clamor of the Falls, you may find a solitary grave, sunken, unkept, the grave-stone leaning like age without a staff, and on the stone a name of foreign flavor—alas! a woman's name besides—and a phrase to tell where she was born across the seas, and when, an ocean between her cradle and her grave, she died. This, no more; yet your eyes will grow wet with tears as you stoop to read the epitaph. A woman lying so alone! And that stranger's grave presents all the pathos of poetry and all the tragedy of life. Small wonder, then, a poet should kindle to pity and sob the woe we feel. Longfellow has caught this somber spirit in his lovely prelude to Hiawatha. Hear him mourn:

> "Ye who sometimes in your rambles
> Through the green lanes of the country,
> Where the tangled barberry-bushes
> Hang their tufts of crimson berries
> Over stone walls gray with mosses,
> Pause by some neglected graveyard,
> For a while to muse and ponder
> On a half-effaced inscription,
> Written with little skill of song-craft,
> Homely phrases, yet each letter
> Full of hope, and yet of heart-break;
> Full of all the tender pathos
> Of the here and the hereafter."

And in this same temper, Gray has wept aloud. The "Elegy in a Country Churchyard" is an exquisite conception, and the execution is as exquisite. He summons all the accessories of grief—ivy-mantled tower, twilight solitude, gloaming in which the dim past with its dead dares walk abroad. Death is a leveler; for life's pomp and power, as its mute, inglorious inconsequence come to a common home. This is what Horace said; this is what history says; and this is what poetry must, in truth, declare. This elegy is somber as an autumn sky. We see the pageant we name life pass like a roseate dream. It glows with morning and high hope; but evening dims the glow and night is here before we thought the day had well begun. In this elegy we are scarcely touched to tears. We are something less.

> "The touch of a vanished hand,
> And the sound of a voice that is still,"

would make us weep; but Gray had not that dower of passion. Fervor slept in his spirit. Impersonal and passionless, what he can do and does is to bring the gray of gloaming over our spirits; and that is a gracious state for thought, and gives it wings. Gray's elegy leaves us in the churchyard.

But "Lycidas," in strong contrast, is intensely personal. The poem is a sob. 'Tis Milton weeps. A college friend is dead, drowned on the seas, but leaves a friend to weep for him, whose lament will give the dead immortality. In the "Elegy in a Country Churchyard," a scholar, a book-lover, a recluse, cons over to himself the story of the flitting pageant men call life. In "Lycidas," a friend mourns for a friend beside the sea, in words sad as the sea's own music. A bereft heart speaks. There is no nobler elegy. "In Memoriam" is sadder, but we hear no nobler music. Some of Milton's grandest strength is evidenced in "Lycidas"—his vigor, his music, as if Milton could ever forget music! It was part of his life. No greater master of musical expression ever attempted putting thought to speech. The word descriptive of Gray's elegy is, "Finished." It is a gem daintily set. "Lycidas" is a gem whose cutting and setting are matters of lesser moment. The gem is rare enough to be a star in a queen's coronet. Not but what "Lycidas" is a finished poem, but that is not its chief excellency. Strength of passion and sublimity of thought speak. Gray's elegy says, "All things end." Milton's elegy says, "To-day dies, but to-morrow dawns." This friend, wrecked on the seas and buried in its blue sepulcher, is not thought of as dead. Immortality is not a phrase, but a fact. His dirge rises into a pæan of triumph. The sobbing ceases, and the voice is as

> "The song of them that triumph,
> The shout of them that feast."

"Lycidas" is written in the Christian temper, and speaks the Christian hope. It does not despair, although it weeps. "Weeping may endure for a night, but joy cometh in the morning." "Lycidas" is an ode framed after the Pauline pattern, in which the shout breaks off the lamentation—"O death, where is thy sting? O grave, where is thy victory?" Such is the destiny of the Christian elegy. It is as a dawn, which forgets its gray in the crimson and glory of sunrise.

And now we listen to another lute. Shelley laments his Adonais. In point of eminence, Shelley's theme—Keats—is worthiest among the elegies; and he has written a noble lament. Shelley was genius, using light for ink; and "Adonais" is in his softer tones. The wild rebellion which spake in "Queen Mab," and in "Prometheus Unbound," is all but silent here. Shelley needed softening. So rare his music, more the pity it grew strident so often. This elegy from the standpoint of poetry is surprisingly beautiful. Those touches for which his hand was noted, are here in affluence. Chaste passages are abundant as violets in springtime. To read is to reread with growing delight. He does not weary, but entices. Genius bewailing genius is not a sight so common as to grow commonplace. It were difficult to conceive a sweeter or more varied expression of grief.

> "Lost echo sits amid the voiceless mountains,
> And feeds her grief with his remembered lay."

> "Grief made the young Spring wild, and she threw down
> Her kindling buds as if she Autumn were,
> Or they dead leaves."

> "And love taught grief to fall like music from his tongue."

Shelley's expression of grief leaves little to be desired, but his earth lacks a sky. He knows no hope, and who lacks hope is a poor comforter to stand beside a grave. Shelley was atheist sometimes, and pantheist at others. His theology, like that of Emerson, was chaotic and variable. "Adonais" is pantheistic, and pantheism is a poor boon to a sorrowing spirit.

> "Death feeds on thy mute voice, and laughs at our despair."

But beside our grave the soul cries out, and will not be silenced. Soul cries, "He is not dead; he could not die." The soul feeds on immortality. So Shelley, the hunger on him, cries:

"Naught we know dies; shall that alone which knows
Be as a sword consumed before the sheath
By sightless lightning?"

"He is made one with nature."

"He is a portion of that loveliness
Which once he made more lovely."

"The One remains, the many change and pass."

You can not well conceive a sadder strain. Hopelessness made vocal. George Eliot's "O, may I join the choir invisible," is of the same temper, though the pantheism is more adroitly hidden. Both voices choke with despair. The antithesis between the triumphant hope of "Lycidas" and the dull despair of "Adonais" is sharp and tragic. The poet to weep beside a grave is he whose vision is so keen as to see beyond it.

Latest begotten of elegies is "In Memoriam." It is the longest, and, all things considered, the noblest elegy man has indited. This is a sob like Rachel weeping for her slain; a cry like David, "O Absalom, my son!" There is no lack of passion here. "In Memoriam" is an argument of human life, and runs the gamut—labor, pain, tragedy, consolation, doubt, faith, endurance, triumph, death, immortality, the passionate beseeching,

> "O would that my tongue could utter
> The thoughts that arise in me!"

The age is mirrored. It glooms with doubt, but brightens into hope at last. Tennyson is no agnostic, but theist; who, though doubts assail and storms beat hard, will still hold in the gloom and tempest, knowing the world to be meaningless and life an irony unless God be hid in history. I think Tennyson eminently exponential, specially so here. He glasses his age. A work of art, be it painting or poem, will probably present two diverse characteristics—the age element and the ageless element—the latter being that fiber of literature which is unchanging and eternal, the former being the contagion of the era. Now, Tennyson belonged to an age when agnosticism was wrestling with faith like some tall giant. "We do not know" is the sad maxim of this pathetic philosophy. If we have God to Father, it is still as if we were in perpetual orphanage. That such philosophy will be somber goes without the saying. The gray evening of a winter's day is not so despairing as such a theory of existence. And in Tennyson is there impress of this dubitative. His larger vision denies the negation; his lesser, fears lest it be true. The words of King Arthur on the mere's marge are indicative of Tennyson's own attitude, "For all my mind is clouded with a doubt." And with this doubt "In Memorian" struggles. A beloved friend is dead—untimely death is a perplexing fact of destiny. "Why, why?" sobs the bereft soul; and no one has put sobs to words and music so graciously as Tennyson.

The poem abounds in nobilities of thought and utterance. It makes articulate the struggle of innumerable souls; and at the last this is the largest service genius performs, to speak our longings, express our pain, give words to our silence, so that we say, "This is my thought." Well, "In Memoriam" has given words to a burdened and a sorrowing heart forever. It can not be dumb any more; and hereafter always the heart will be beholden to Alfred Tennyson. Nor has he uttered simply a cry of pain, but has constructed a philosophy of life.

"We have but faith; we can not know"—

this keys the music of this elegy. Yet God is. Here is great certainty:

"Our little systems have their day,
  They have their day and cease to be;
  They are but broken lights of thee,
And Thou, O Lord, art more than they!"

So far the prelude; but the poem launches into the deep of its theme in words like these:

"I hold it truth with him who sings
  To one clear harp in divers tones,
  That men may rise on stepping-stones
Of their dead selves to higher things."

He raises the profound question of the use of suffering, and the "far-off interest of tears." "Never morning wore to evening but some heart did break;" and his cause of woe is,

"My Arthur, whom I shall not see
Till all my widowed race be run."

But concludes:

"I hold it true whate'er befall,
  I feel it when I sorrow most;
  'T is better to have loved and lost,
Than never to have loved at all."

The poet's hope is, We shall not die. There is no melting into nature as with Shelley, but assured immortality:

> "My own dim life should teach me this,
>   That life shall live for evermore,
>   Else earth is darkness at the core,
> And dust and ashes all that is."

Though dead, this friend is not forgotten:

> "And dear to me, as sacred wine
>   To dying lips, is all he said."

'T is immortality is very sure:

> "There no shade shall last
>   In that deep dawn behind the tomb;"

> "And I shall know him when we meet,
>   And we shall sit at endless feast
>   Enjoying each the other's good."

Then doubt breaks into hope, and dulls its glow:

> "I falter where I firmly trod,
>   And falling with my weight of cares
>   Upon the great world's altar-stairs,
>   That slope through darkness up to God."

It was

> "God's finger touched him, and he slept."

Doubt shall not wrest away his hope:

"If e'er when faith had fallen asleep,
  I heard a voice, 'Believe no more,'
  And heard an ever-breaking shore
That tumbled in the Godless deep:

A warmth within the breast would melt
  The freezing reason's colder part,
  And, like a man in wrath, the heart
Stood up, and answered, 'I have felt.'"

And at the closing of this greatest elegy, the poet, like a swimmer who, shipwrecked, has battled with the sea and overcome its might and wrath, calls:

"That God which ever lives and loves—
  One God, one law, one element,
  And one far-off, Divine event,
To which the whole creation moves."

And in that conclusion we join as participants in triumph. The battle was not ours, but ours the victory. And in the poet's groping, his catching sight of God, his glooms that all but conquer hope, his holding still to the great God till, in the end, God breaks upon him like a sea,—this struggle and this triumph are for us.

So run the elegies. Gray leaves us in the churchyard; Shelley gives us back to airs and earth; Tennyson will have soul

> "Climb the great world's altar-stairs,
> That slope through darkness up to God;"

And Milton, without a hush of doubt, shouts "Immortality!"

The Soliloquies of Macbeth and Hamlet

SPEECH is thinking aloud. Soliloquy is thinking aloud to one's self. A monologue, such as was a conversation or lecture of Coleridge, is nothing other than a soliloquy. When a soul is absorbed in itself and its concerns, be that soul alone or in company, there will be no surprise if it speak for its own ears. In this fact is a unique psychological condition. Since the soul is conversant with its own reasonings, why speak? If we do not purpose the impartation of truth to another, why coin thinking into words? Yet is this a common ailment. You will have observed, a child thinks aloud; and age is like to do the same. And in the normal state of soul, when life is oppressed, when the vastest issues break like angry oceans in the spirit—then thoughts seem bent on uttering themselves. The spirit, oblivious to all things save its own interests, babbles as a brook, though the voice is scarce audible to the speaker's own ears. *Absorbed* is the condition of the soliloquy; and it is easy to see that a soul in stress will tend to this form of utterance.

Such is the state of Macbeth and Hamlet. They are unlike, as if they inhabited different stars. One is soldier, the other civilian. Macbeth is the man of action, Hamlet the man of thought. With Macbeth, the sword is the native speech; with Hamlet, words are drawn daggers. Macbeth is matured manhood; Hamlet is youth with despair tugging at the heart, and watching at the eyes. In these tragedies, Shakespeare works at the antipodes. He shapes two spirits so diverse as to seem creations of two brains, rather than one,—Macbeth the soldier, and Hamlet the thinker. A soldier! A man whose argument is war, whose soul intones its speech to battle tumult; to whom march or foray, wild charge or passionless beleaguerment, defeat or triumph, are the articulate voices of the soul. Arms dazzle. The battle thunder bewilders, confounds, maddens, makes heroic. In the soldier is something tense, like a bent bow. He is perpetually on the verge of heroisms. The soldier is restless in peace. War is his joy. It soothes his spirit, as the caress of a fair hand a sick man's pulse. In war, he is alive. His every faculty is alert. His ear catches whispers. His eyes sweep the hills to the far blue. He sees all.

The battle trumpet sets his blood on fire. Unwittingly to himself his hand will finger his sword hilt. Prince Maurice of Nassau will be lost when battle ceases. William of Orange will drop his mask and glow like a lover when battle thickens about him like winter's storm. The soldier's dream is action; and Macbeth was a soldier.

Hamlet was thinker. He was a lad at college. Philosophy intoxicated him as rare wine. His was a Platonic mind. Thoughts filled his sky thicker than the stars. Life seemed to him a chance for constructing philosophies. See Plato and Kant and Hegel, how their world revolves within their study walls! Life was thought, not action. Swords are toys. Battles are bagatelles. Life's grave and eager ministry is to think, to build immortalities by intellection; to sight the world's pageant as if a shadow floated o'er the hills. The shadows are poor temporalities; the hills alone are eternal. So will the thinker underrate the actor, who, to him, seems lacking in depth. His life runs on the surface as bubbles. Plato will at heart pity Themistocles; and Aristotle will think Alexander's conquests tawdry; and Hegel will marvel Napoleon did not prefer philosophy to imperial sway. The soldier and thinker, the achiever and conceiver, stand at opposite quarters of the sky, like sunrise and sunset. Name them Macbeth and Hamlet. Such is Shakespeare's bold attempt. He will create the dreamer and achiever. And of him who created Falstaff and King Lear, who can say this to be beyond his powers?

Now, in consonance with this *motif* of these tragedies is the totality of scheme and movement. They never forget. In no display of his surprising powers has Shakespeare shown himself so much the incomparable genius. In Hamlet action never really wakes: in Macbeth action never sleeps. Events drive like a whirlwind. Movement is everywhere. Events march as the army of which Macbeth was commander. You note progress, because the movement marches past you. Events trample on each other's heels. The witch's hell-broth, the dawn of illicit desire for kingship, the mounting the steps that lead to the throne; some black as night, some slippery with blood, and all with the shame of crime upon them—treason, murders, suspicions, flights, conspiracies, remorse, defeats, follow fast like waves toward a shore. You are caught in the vortex.

of events. There is a maelstrom of movement. The contagion of action fires your blood. That is the drama of Macbeth.

But Hamlet is becalmed. It looks to achievement, but does not reach it. Incident there is, but no action. We leave matters as we find them, so far as concerns a purpose. Polonius dies of a chance sword-thrust. Ophelia, delirious for love, lies dead in the shadowed stream. Hamlet and Laertes die of poisoned foil-thrust. Queen Gertrude drinks poisoned wine meant for Hamlet; and King Claudius alone is slain by purposed action of the prince. Aside from this, all are happenings, and, in a true sense, that, too, is happening, since he was stung to it by his own murder through the king's plan. The play lacks the quality of achievement. Hamlet planned to avenge his father's death, but knew not how to compass it; and the tragedy dies on the threshold of action. Coleridge has given us truth in his acute criticism. Hamlet is no doer, but is betrayed into action. Macbeth the doer; Hamlet the dreamer.

Now knowing Macbeth and Hamlet, we may anticipate their soliloquies. Macbeth will be objective, Hamlet subjective. One strikes against a foe; the other meditates striking himself. Between Macbeth's thought and resolution there is not a hairbreadth space. Between Hamlet and action is the breadth of a world. Yet, strange as it may seem, Hamlet passes into soliloquy not easier than Macbeth. The man of action and the man of thought, each with burdened spirit, con their thoughts aloud. Tremendous passions speak in each, and passion has one language and one method.

In Macbeth's soliloquy, you always feel action hangs on the skirts of thought. In Act I, Scene v, the soliloquy is big with action. Threats leap from his eyes. And in Scene vii Macbeth is still true to his dominating idea:

"If it were done when 't is done, then 't were well
It were done quickly."

"Do," "do," that is his word. His sword is ready, his fingers on the hilt; look to see it leap from its scabbard. Observe, the *deed* is uppermost. No introspection is visible. The deed and its consequences fill the mind, like waters, to the brim. In Act II, Scene i, the thought is objective:

"Is this a dagger which I see before me,
The handle toward my hand?"

And the dagger is for Duncan. He meditates striking for kingdom. There is menace in his suggestion; and his look at the dagger-handle bodes the sleeping Duncan ill. Were the soliloquy on Hamlet's lips, Duncan might sleep quiet as a child, and dream no harm; but since it is Macbeth thinking aloud, Duncan, Ho! Let danger's nightmare wake thee from thy sleep! Death stumbles toward thee in the dark! In Act II, Scene ii, the conversation between husband and wife has the seeming of a monologue rather than a dialogue, and still has movement. "Macbeth does murder sleep." Macbeth is always *doing*. In Scene i of Act III, Macbeth plans death once more. Now it is Banquo. His ambition and his sword know not to sleep. In Scene iii of Act V is Macbeth's last soliloquy. Doom comes toward him; clouds his sky, makes dark his noon; yet is he not changed. He is doer still. To hold his own amid outnumbering foes, this is his dream. He is the soldier yet.

"My way of life
Is fallen into the sere, the yellow leaf."

Curses, not honor, his portion—but still a king! And scepter and sword will he hold till death shall wrench them from him.

"Why should I play the Roman fool and die
  On mine own sword? Whiles I see lives, the gashes
Do better upon them."

Such is this soldier king; and when he dies, 't is fighting. He and action are sworn friends. Certain it is, Macbeth is consistent with himself in life and death.

In Hamlet are four *bona fide* soliloquies. These occur, one in Act I, two in Act III, and one in Act IV; while besides, in Act II, Hamlet's rejoinder to Guildenstern is not so much reply as soliloquy. Soliloquy is natural to Hamlet as turbulence to the seas. His conversations are monologues. He takes other men's words as points of departure. He deals in dissertations, not conversations. Yet, how singular and acute the Shakespearean treatment! If Hamlet fall into soliloquy as naturally as stars fall with flash-light to the earth at night, yet is he still more the brooder than the soliloquizer. His lips do not often catch his heart's words. He will be quiet. Macbeth has given him over to soliloquy as frequently as Hamlet; and here is Shakespeare right as always. Hamlet's mood is to think, to dream, rather than speak in whispers even. He will hide his passion. Not even Horatio shall know his heart.

But play you the eavesdropper. Hear Hamlet count his woes as the nun her beads. In Act I he meditates, though remotely, self-slaughter. He faults the world.

> " 'T is an unweeded garden
> That grows to seed."

'T is "weary, stale, flat, and unprofitable." 'T is a dreary waste, littered with shame and broken hopes and mouthing fears. Having his mother in his thought, he moans, "Frailty, thy name is woman!" His soliloquy is a moan, but has no movement. The end finds him no nearer suicide than the beginning. Nay, he is further removed. He has forgotten his main thesis. But that the world turns him sick in looking at it, we can not argue.

In Act III, he still has suicide at heart, but is drawing nearer to it. At the first approach he does but lament, because the Almighty "has fixed his canon against self-slaughter." Now

the view is positive, "To be, or not to be."
The point of a bared bodkin gleams before his
thought. Death and he are touching hands.
But 't is thought, not action. The reasons
against outtop the reasons for. Hamlet recedes from suicide now as before. But further,
in Act III, he thinks aloud in his own hearing.
Now he passes from thought of self-slaughter
to that of slaughtering the king. Seeing Claudius praying, breathing hard he whispers,

"Now might I do it pat, now he is praying."

But if Claudius be slain at prayer, then shall
he, by Hamlet's logic, come to heaven; hence
he will not kill him thus.

"But when he is drunk asleep, or in his rage,
. . . .
Then trip him that his heels may kick at heaven,
And that his soul may be as damned and black
As hell, whereto it goes."

These conditions are not met; and action is
as far removed as when thought began. Not
yet, wait—that is the conclusion. Once more,
in Act IV, hear Hamlet soliloquize. He still
dreams of action. He is haunted by the purpose to slay the king. His thought cries,

Now! Now! but his hand holds back. There is no contagion between thought and sword. He is brave as Achilles. Cowardice is no fault to be charged against Hamlet. But thought is not action. He sees himself derelict. Duty cries, Slay the king! All actions do but argue and augment the royal guilt, and mark the royal criminal a target for an angry sword; and as Hamlet goes from us, hear him say,

"From this time forth
My thoughts be bloody or be nothing worth."

Yet are action and Hamlet far apart as are the Pole Star and the Southern Cross.

If you will compare the chief soliloquies of Macbeth and Hamlet, and bring the conclusion into small compass, you shall see the men as by a flash of lightning in the night.

Macbeth has a dagger before him; Hamlet meditates on a bare bodkin. Hamlet means the bodkin for his own breast; Macbeth the dagger for another's heart. "To be, or not to be," says Hamlet; "To do, or not to do," says Macbeth. One thinks, and drifts farther from his purpose: O, that is Hamlet! One thinks, springs to his feet, grasps dagger-hilt, and drives it surely home; and this is Macbeth. Hamlet will soliloquize on suicide; Macbeth will not entertain the thought, though adversity drive broken sword against his breast. Hear him upon the battle-field spurn the thought of self-murder. Hear Hamlet meditate on assassinating Claudius. He pricks his own slow purpose. He dreams to do, and does not. Had life given him a longer day, he had avenged Hamlet the ghost;

> "But the native hue of resolution
> Is sickled o'er with the pale cast of thought."

But Macbeth the soldier is steeped in crime ere his plans are well matured. Duncan, Banquo, armed conspiracies—he is against them all. He drives against them like a charge of cavalry. He can not sit and think; but he can do and die.

And Hamlet lying white and dead upon the sands of Elsinore; and Macbeth at Dunsinane fighting as fiends fight or heroes, there slain and borne a trophy to the rightful king—Hamlet and Macbeth—far apart in life, are by the same sword brought to death. Thinker and actor lie silent in one grave.

The Ebb Tide

THERE is art in naming a novel. Scott found this his chief difficulty; but how admirably he succeeded let his titles attest. Cooper was ultimately compelled to change the caption of his first attempt at fiction. Marion Crawford was so taken with the name of a woman he met that he wrote asking her consent to make it the title of his forthcoming novel; and, she consenting, we have "Katherine Lauderdale." That a work may survive a bad title is no refutation of the claim here made. A sorrier caption than Besant's "All Sorts and Conditions of Men" is hard to conceive; but the volume is virile enough to survive in spite of the ill christening. There is a euphony of name naturally appealing to the mind. "The Prisoner of Zenda" is a captivating title, as well as a captivating book. "Geoffrey Hamlyn" is well named. "Quentin Durward," "Ivanhoe," "Henry Esmond," "Lorna Doone," "Ben Hur," are all well-chosen titles. But when the theme of a novel is not a proper name, but a phrase, the art becomes more involved. A good title conceals meaning, excites interest, and when the book is done should justify itself by its appositeness. "The Ebb Tide" answers these demands. It gives no hint of meaning, makes picture of the evening sea, rouses involuntary questioning, and when the story is ended satisfies the reader as being the exact name for such a tale. "The Ebb Tide" is a metaphor. The sea has no bearing on the fiction. Not an ebbing tide is mentioned in the volume. The reference is to life, and not to seas; and when reviewed in thought compasses a pathos of meaning deeper than the silences which underlie the lapping tides of ocean.

The story is not involved. No digressions or halts for the introduction of new episodes or new characters, as in "Martin Chuzzlewit" or "Middlemarch." The tale keeps straight on like a traveler in unhindered journey. The characters are few. Love has no part in the passing pageant. The book is fiction in form; but, more's the pity, is truth's story retold. We are haunted by the memory, knowing it is not a dream, but a late recorded history of many unwritten lives. We can not put the pathos from us. It clings like shadow to the mountain. This work is grown out of the soil of Stevenson's health-exile in Samoa. Doubtless, on the wharves of that far island in the South Seas, he had seen the men whose biographies are here written down.

The story is this: "Robert Herrick was the son of an intelligent, active, and ambitious man, small partner in a considerable London house. Hopes were conceived of the boy." He was sent to Oxford, and had taste and talent, "but was deficient in consistency and intellectual manhood." He dabbled in Greek and music and mathematics. His fault was the fault of many—lack of integrity of plan. The father failing in business, the son was thrown on his own resources; became a clerk and despised his vocation, feeling himself above it. He was honest, courteous, and useless. He did not drink. He had no distinctive vice; but his "course was one unbroken shame." He was worthless to his employers. Talents he had, but application none. He ceases writing home, and thus cuts himself off from his sole anchorage. He can keep no employment long; is buffeted, not by fortune, but by his own inaction and incapacity. He leaves America, and sails to the islands of the South Seas, where food requires scarce an effort in securing, and where shelter and clothing are neither elaborate nor costly. Besides, there men had climbed to be "queen's consorts and king's ministers." But Herrick changes his name, which certifies his lack of manful purpose. The biographer says wisely, "The *alias* betrayed his moral bankruptcy." A place got was lost; and he fails to get bread. This was a habit now. He exhausts credit, he begs; repulsed, he prefers starvation or digs his food from rubbish heaps, his bedroom a disused prison; his companions—one a villain, vain, boastful, vulgar; the other, generous-hearted, weak, drunken, occupationless, ambitionless, but still a man whose hand it was not a shame to take. How low is the man of fine fiber and fair parts fallen! He sees his estate, blushes in the darkness, revolts, but is quiescent. Burnt with heat by day, shivering with cold by night, starving, a parasite, threatened with arrest as a vagabond, feeling his shame,—this is Herrick. His failures incapacitate him for success. He meditates suicide, for his moral nature is a wreck.

A ship flying a yellow flag at the mast sails into port. Smallpox has slain a drunken captain and mate. The seaman is, default of better material, made captain. Herrick becomes first mate. The captain purposes the theft of cargo and vessel. Herrick is indignant, protests, yields; but on the voyage as the captain and the clerk—associates in poverty and shame on the island beach—sink in drunken revels which are continuous, he plays the man, pilots the ship, feels terrible disgust, and rising indignation. By mismanagement in a squall the captain all but wrecks the ship. Herrick, outraged and angry, is ready for death. The ship, with victualing gone, drifts into an unknown port, held by a white man of commanding person and imposing spirit, a strange character, but a man gifted to rule, and a pearl merchant with unknown wealth of pearls hid in his safe. He is drawn to Herrick, but despises the two associates, and shows it. He reads them all, as if they were open books written in a known tongue. He senses the scholar in Herrick, pities and despises his weakness. Captain Davis, and Huish the clerk, resent the undisguised contempt of the island lord, and plan his murder, the seizing of his wealth, the victualing their ship, and the sailing home to opulence and content.

Herrick, though weak and a consort of thieves, is not a villain. He knows not what to do. Feeling himself a criminal, sharer in a stolen ship, his moral stamina counts for little. Despising his companions, he still feels the tug of association. Can he betray his friends? He feels he can not. Dare he see this sometime host of theirs foully murdered? He dare not. How can these conflicting claims be adjusted? And a weak man gives a weak man's answer—suicide. He leaps into the bay, and finding himself afraid to die, makes his way shoreward, and sits dripping on the sand nauseated with himself. *He can not even die.* Humiliated, shamed, with the spell of his fatal indecision still on him, the island magnate finds him, and he becomes a dependent of this strong man, letting another will do what his has not done. Huish lands, approaches the man he hates, holds up his hands; but in one hides a bottle of vitriol, which he purposes throwing in his enemy's face, but is detected, attempts to throw, and, as the bottle leaves his hand, Atwater's Winchester shatters it, and the vitriol boils down on his own face. Another bullet ends the wretch. Davis stands apart appalled. Herrick sees the tragedy; and the tale leaves him hopeless, lost.

Tragic enough this fiction is. Not a hint of humor nor a glint of sunshine in the book from lid to lid. Somber, pathetic! This is no story to read for rest and pleasure. No comedy laughs on any page. Here is succession of shadows. Shakespeare will smile even beside the grave; not so Stevenson.

This work is a collaboration. The name of Osbourne shares the title-page with Stevenson. How large his contribution, we are not told; but I think it clear the result is more satisfactory than such partnerships usually produce. Literary partnerships sin against personality. We care to feel a writer's heart. His selfhood ought to be the background of every page. This sense of individuality an associate authorship destroys. But it is safe to say that in "The Ebb Tide" Stevenson has been the master-spirit. His genius is in the plan. His rare English flashes like light from the pages; and to write a critique of the novel in the name of Stevenson's known characteristics seems just.

I mention three characteristics of Stevenson's genius. These are: Exquisite English, lack of love as a factor in his fictions, and the somberness of his art.

The English of Robert Louis Stevenson is a perpetual delight. His style, at its best, is music. As a simple study in language, "Dr. Jekyl and Mr. Hyde" is to me a growing wonder. The "New Arabian Nights" is a piece of enchanting verbiage. His felicity of speech, his lucidity, his spontaneity, his naturalness and ease, conspire to make him a prose poet. To read his best productions is a growing joy, because new beauty reveals itself at every step. I read him as I would sit in autumn and watch a mountain stream go laughing in crystal tangles down the hills, and standing in quiet pools to mirror sky and cloud. I never tire. The beauty abides. Stevenson's English is that mountain stream a-journey toward the deep. Take this extract from Robert Herrick's farewell letter to his sweetheart: "Turn the key in the door; let no thought of me return; be done with the poor ghost that pretended he was a man, and stole your love." Or this: "I have no more to say; only linger going out, like an unwilling guest."

Stevenson's art makes little of love. It

makes more of Mars than Eros. His are novels of battle. The struggle element is uppermost. With Dickens, Thackeray, Hall Caine, Blackmore, the love element is nodal. It is not so with Stevenson. Either adventure or tragic effort is the central actor. Run over in thought the novels of the author under discussion, and you will observe how unvaryingly true this criticism is. "The Ebb Tide" is no exception. A fascinating novel, not a story of adventure, runs its course, and, save by bare intimation, love has no voice, no beauty of affection to cast its spell over us. That we read a book of this sort with sustained interest is a high tribute to the author. He entices us to study decadence of character. With chaste verbiage, with accurate delineation, with clear adhesion to the central subject, with interest growing as the pages multiply,—thus are we held. There is undoubted mastery here. And Stevenson must be ranked among the major novelists. It is with soul struggles he deals, though not with manly conquests.

His genius is essentially somber. Frequently, to use a term indigenous to his native land, it is "uncanny." He will write only tragedy. Sunshine, if it play on the pages of his creations, darkens in a moment. Perhaps his constant ill-health may be offered as explanatory, at least in part. I am of opinion that between Stevenson and Edgar Allan Poe there is a distinct spirit of resemblance. Poe's tales are terrible and graphic, realistic as DeFoe, tragic as the "Scarlet Letter," mystical as "Kubla Khan," and lurid with genius. My conviction is that more than an apparent similarity exists between the tales of Poe and those of Stevenson. The "New Arabian Nights" and "The Strange Case of Dr. Jekyl and Mr. Hyde" are definitely like Poe in their flavor. They are extravagant and terrible. Stevenson, whether by intent or not, is pessimistic. "Virginibus Puerisque," that series of essays written in such spotless English, leaves a not altogether pleasant flavor on the lip. In this regard his works do really belie him. He was true, tender, loving. But that impress rests on all. His books deal with evil in character. Nothing cheery or heroic emanates from them. "The Master of Ballantrae," perhaps his most virile contribution to fiction, is one increasing gloom. Tragic at its inception, it is mad with horror at its close. "Kidnapped" is graphic as if written with lightning on a sky at night,

but depressing as the shadow of a grave. The
"Misadventures of John Nicholson" is a procession of sufferings and mistakes, with scarce
a memory of mellow light. "Dr. Jekyl and
Mr. Hyde" is as gruesome and dispiriting as
can well be pictured. It closes in shadows and
the night. There is a shadow on every landscape. The ruddy hues of Burns find no answering glow in Stevenson. His is a genius
gloomy as a Scotch glen.

In this regard, then, "The Ebb Tide" is
native to the author. But we are not to infer
that, because gloomy, he is unnatural. Stevenson is no dreamer. He is exact. Accuracy
is characteristic of his creations. Scott verified
his landscapes and battle-grounds by a tour
of investigation. Stevenson verified his portraitures by observation keen as a Roman
stylus. His is no haphazard movement. If
he will give us tragedy and not comedy, know
that tragedy is an every-day commodity.
Life's processes do not all terminate in joy.
Tears mix their wine for many a lip. The case
of Jekyl and Hyde is historical as Cæsar Borgia or Lorenzo the Magnificent. The history
of evil sheltered, is good turned from the door
into the stormy night. Stevenson is logical.

He lets sin work to its own conclusion. Hyde is hellish, but natural and familiar. The type of life our author gives portrait of is not a myth. Would it were. "The Master of Ballantrae" is accurate portraiture. The characteristics therein mentioned may be traced in many a family history. The shameful when written is never palatable. Sin is hideous. That is what Jekyl and Hyde means. That is what "The Master of Ballantrae" means. That is what the pirate captain in "Treasure Island" means. That is what Huish in "The Ebb Tide" means. This Scotch novelist has a lesson to teach if we can hear. And "The Ebb Tide," melancholy as the story is, is a drama of life. A weak man becomes worthless and a parasite and a criminal. He was not libertine nor drunkard, murderer nor taker of gold; but he became base for all. What meaning is here? What is the interpretation of this handwriting on the wall? Let the author give it in his own words: "It is not enough to say, 'I will be base.'" Weakness is badness. To do wrong, it is not necessary to have a plan of wickedness. Good is affirmative. Not to do good is to do evil. This man, with a scholar's love and longing; with his tattered Virgil

giving him solace in hours barren of joy; with
his memory of rare music, once heard, never
forgotten; with his instincts for the better, and
his inward detestation of beggary and crime,—
he, with memory of the woman he loved fresh,
unfading; with love of his home and its dear
company drawing him like a magnet, with eye
for beauty of beach and cloud and sweep of
sea; with the virtues speaking in his ears like
rare music,—with all of this, he was fallen.
Nay, he had even *tried*. Struggle he had
known. He was sinking as a man in a bog, who
watches the silent waste suck him down inch
by inch. There is deep pathos here. The author has given us reality, and we supposed we
read fiction. Lassitude was Herrick's sin.
One mighty wrestle, one battle into which he
had flung the strength of his life, and he had
been saved! And he knew that, but would
not make the struggle. His will became enervated. At the first he could have changed his
career with comparative ease. But he accustomed himself to defeat, and bore it meekly.
He kissed the hand that smote him, till at the
end sloth became a habit, and incertitude
sapped his vitality. He lost confidence in himself, and hope for himself. Can you conceive

Galiatt in "Toilers of the Sea" a poltroon and a beggar? Why, Galiatt defied sea and death. He warred with the inevitable, and conquered. Heroisms are in reach of all. No monopolies are tolerated here. What Galiatt was, Herrick might have been. And he knew it! That was his passionless despair. Seeing all gone, he felt he might have retained it as a woman sees her lover pass from her, knowing a word, a cry in the gathering darkness, would bring him back,—but does not utter it. "He might have been!" That haunted him like a voice of love. He could not be deaf to it. And such a man lying a rag upon the shore! Pity, pity! and only himself to blame! If he could have flung defiance, crying, "I could do no other, I was overborne," then had he rested as a man made prisoner in battle outnumbered by foes. The sense of having done our utmost, upholds like an amazing strength. Herrick knew better. He knew whose fault it was that he, an Oxford scholar, was unknown, unloved, an outcast in a foreign land under an alien sky, asked the alms of bread. There lay his pain. To know good, is not of necessity to do good; and the tide receded! Ebb Tide!

God's ocean tides come back and wash the shores again. But life's tide not so. It slips back, goes out, and power passes from us. There is menace in a lapping tide. A moment more, the ebb begins! Robert Herrick made himself the thing he was. Meant for manhood, he made himself fit only for servitude. Some larger spirit than his must command. He knew only to obey. The passing of a soul, this is the drama we have viewed.

The two potent factors in destiny are self and God. This man made use of neither. Himself lay as an unused oar. And God? He gives no thought to him. What a fatal omission! We have no hint in all the history that he even knew of God. Reared in a Christian land, he must have known God, but discloses no belief in him nor any recognition of him. To all intents he was atheist. Himself but weakness, he knew no larger strength than his. He being as he was, and ignoring the Supreme strength, what could ensue but weakness? Stranded like a ship touched by no wave, with only a memory of buoyant seas upon it—that was Robert Herrick; and the ebb tide would come back no more!

Somber this book is as a rainy autumn evening; but we have read the tragedy of a wasted life, and how could sunlight break in on such a scene? "The Ebb Tide" should pass into the curriculum of reading for every youth and maid. A tale of shipwreck, it is as full of warning as the night that broods above the sea of moaning voices.

The Jew in Fiction

THE Jew is the romance of history. Oldest of living peoples; with authentic kingdom before battle trumpeted at the gate of Troy, whose ten tribes passed into perpetual banishment when Greece and Rome were mythic names and waging mythic wars; with history and genius, unprecedented longevity and unparalleled catastrophe, the solitary people to whose annals miracles indubitably belong, the race to which our world owes its chief monotheistic systems—a race whose personality has not been impaired by vast attrition, half of which reduced the Roman race to a shadowy, though colossal memory—the Jew is this day sole survivor of the ancient world, and the miracle of history. With the Jew this article concerns itself.

And what a name to conjure with! From Israel sprung Abraham and David, Moses and Solomon, Elijah and Isaiah and Spinoza, Saul of Tarsus and Jesus of Nazareth. A plant capable of bursting into such bloom must have been watered with dews from heaven.

One can not well fix thought upon the Hebrew without beginning to dream. His career has been so thrilling, and his virility appears so unimpaired, as to waken expectations concerning his future. When summer is past, and winter winds begin to blow, we cherish no hope of flowers. We know their day is dead. But the Jew seems not to be on the verge of winter, but rather on the verge of spring. The winds that blow in his face, though cold, are yet freighted with the fragrance of a growing world. That a race should have survived the wreck of thirty centuries and catastrophes unparalleled in history, and yet have no triumphant morrow, seems more than incredible.

Novelists are what Hamlet called players, "the abstract and brief chronicle of the time." These are historians of a period whose art makes the era a perpetual life. Of them, historians have found it needful to learn. To make history live is the art of Herodotus, Macaulay, and Francis Parkman. This the novelist is an adept in doing. He belongs to an age. He glasses its life, as a pool the flag and willows along its banks. His estimate of conditions will be impersonal. In his estimate of social values, he belongs to his age, as waves to a shore. He is not originative, but reiterative. And the large place recent writers of fiction (in prose or verse), have given the Jew, is proof of how large a place in thought he occupies, and the attention given him and his tragic history. Earlier English kings were wont to pull the teeth of Jews for pastime; but Queen Victoria has knighted Moses Montefiore; and her reign has seen the first Jew raised to the lord mayorship of London. If, as we may legitimately do, we are to judge from the novelists, the day for undervaluing the Jew is past, as is the day of his persecution. Time was when he was hissed, cursed, burned, broken on the wheel, banished, or, at the kindest, ignored. He has outlived contumely, and has projected himself into the world's thought. Indeed, the last and hardest thing has always been to ignore him; for, in some sense, he was central wherever he was even a temporary citizen. God has thrown round him a flame, so that, as the burning bush, he is not destroyed.

In the British Museum, among its most treasured holdings, is the Portland vase, noblest antique remaining of ancient ceramic art. Were it of solid gold, fetched in some royal

galleon, shaped by some artist of renown, and
carven with arabesques, cunning, intricate, inimitable, wonderful, it would not be the precious thing it is. You may find it now guarded
jealously like king's jewels. Above its solitariness as noblest survival of a noble art,
stands this other fact—the vase is a reconstruction. In other years, a madman flung to
the floor and shattered this bit of fashioned
clay. To-day, however, in a smaller room devoted to itself, as if it were a royal person, the
Portland vase stands as if no maniac's madness
had reduced it to fragments. Put together
thus cunningly, you would not guess calamity
had reduced it to a ruin. And the value of
this vase is enhanced, rather than subtracted
from, by this disaster. Now the Portland vase,
as reproduced from chaos, required the cementing all parts into a whole. No tiniest
chip, splintered by the fall, but finds place in
this survival of classic pottery. In like manner we shall need to reconstruct the Jew as
a type from all fragments accessible. He will
not be adequately pictured by any single artist.
He is too many-sided, and will no more be
limned by one romancist than woman will,
and for the same reason. There are facets

innumerable. Who would know woman, will not find it suffice to acquaint himself with Imogen and Enid and Colombe, but must meet Fatima and Vivien, and Mistress Quickly enamored of Sir John Falstaff. So he who would know the Jew, must see him best and worst; must meet him in the Ghetto as well as in the Rialto; in rags and as minister to kings, the villain Anathoth, and the hero Simonides. What this paper proposes, is a study of this intricate and fascinating character from the following works: Browning's "Holy-cross Day," "Rabbi Ben Ezra," and "Saul;" Kingsley's "Hypatia," Scott's "Ivanhoe," Lessing's "Nathan the Wise," Wallace's "Prince of India" and "Ben Hur," Sue's "Wandering Jew," Zangwill's "Children of the Ghetto," Eliot's "Daniel Deronda," and Caine's "The Scapegoat." You will note that the period of study runs through three centuries, from the writing of "Merchant of Venice" at the close of the sixteenth century, to the close of the nineteenth century and "The Children of the Ghetto." And the landscape on which this Jew appears, extends from the earlier Christian centuries in "Hypatia," to the latest hour in Zangwill.

As a scene sweeps before you, some impression is inseparable from the whole. You name it beautiful or dreary or sublime. So with these fictions. They give a general sense. Diverse the characters as a desert from the Vale of Tempe, yet is there a landscape still. The Jew stands before you, the Orient flushing his face, his thousands of years sitting lightly upon him, leaving no wrinkle on his brow, and you feel, "I have met strength this day." You are sensible of having come in contact with a great character. The mightiest act of a race is its test of power, as the farthest flight of an arrow is measure of a bowman's strength. And we may safely infer, from what pre-eminence fiction gives him, that the Jew projects above the horizons as mountains do.

Browning's "Holy-cross Day" is vivid as sunset tints. This artist brush neither forgets nor fails. It conceives and executes with exact fidelity. This poem may stand for a picture of the mediæval Jew, wronged, helpless, despised, bending to the storm as trees do, but dogged, determined, unchanged at heart. He no more coalesces with his age than oil and water mix. He is in it, but not of it; and seeming to yield, he is, in fact, as unyielding as rocky coast to turbulent waves. That lowering brow, that muttered malediction, that barely concealed hatred of the cross and Christ,—this is the Jew. Hints of his weakness and his strength are here. We pity, but can scarcely admire. His ragged defiance juts into the sea; for his yielding was make-believe. He hates, and is hated; but will, in some measure, subordinate principle to policy. He has protean adjustability. In "Filippo Baldinucci on Burial," you shall see a superior delineation of that hatred toward the Jew which made him gall in hate. If hate were fierce, we can scarcely wonder or blame, since occasion was so pregnant with enmities.

Of "Jochanan Hakkadosh," rabbi, old, sedate, wisdom's ruddiest wine, dying, questioned and listened to by disciples, who hung upon his words as on strong cables,—he is pessimist, worst of pessimists because old, and because to him life has told its story through. Love, battle, learning, each in its turn is declared failure; nor need we wonder when we note God falls not in his category of life events. He, a rabbi, should above all have made dying mention of a Shepherd who had been rod and staff to comfort and defend. The sense of

God at hand redeems us from the shame of despondency at life. But Rabbi Ben Ezra is antidote to Jochanan Hakkadosh. He is a soul poised and strong. We feel the hid strength of him, and we are helped. Rabbi Ben Ezra is old, but optimist. He interprets life's meaning rightly, and is not disappointed; neither seeing death is he afraid. With him "The best is yet to be." He will

> "Welcome each rebuff
> That turns earth's smoothness rough,
> Each sting that bids not sit nor stand, but go!
> Be our joys three parts pain!
> Strive and hold cheap the strain;
> Learn nor account the pang; dare, never grudge the throe."

Clearly, here is a man who has found this world's meaning. Earth is a place to grow manhood; and manhood is cheap at any price. Life seems good to him.

> "Let us not always say,
> 'Spite of this flesh to-day
> I strove, made head, gained ground upon the whole!'
> As the bird wings and sings,
> Let us cry, 'All good things
> Are ours, nor soul helps flesh more than flesh helps soul!'

Therefore, I summon age
To grant youth's heritage,
Life's struggle having so far reached its term:
Thence shall I pass, approved
A man for aye removed
From the developed brute; a God though in the germ."

"Wait death nor be afraid!"
For
"All that is at all
Lasts ever, past recall;
Earth changes, but thy soul and God stand sure:
What entered into thee,
That was, is, and shall be:
Time's wheel runs back or stops: potter and clay endure.

So take and use Thy work,
Amend what flaws may lurk,
What strain o' the stuff, what warpings past the aim!
My times be in Thy hand!
Perfect the cup as planned!
Let age approve of youth, and death complete the same!"

It is better to drink from this cup of Rabbi Ben Ezra than to drink rare Falernian. His age ends as age should, a glad look backward, but a gladder look forward! He is the Jewish doctor, grave, sagacious, learned, provident of good. We seem listening to high-priest Aaron in a monologue. Rabbi Ben Ezra has seen far, and rightly. His have been eagle's eyes. Great truths have swung their suns into his firmament. In his greater moods, he is surely the son of Abraham, and leaves his lesser self abased, his major self exalted, speaking, eloquent.

Saul is unique and noble. The waking of a lethargic soul on contact with youth, vision, genius, faith, is the theme. David, in poem and history, presents both pomp and power of Israel's story. His name pronounced, wakes Israel from the dead. That graceful warrior-poet, untwining lilies from his harp and letting music drip from finger-tips, is a sight we care to keep before our eyes forever. David, a voice for souls—has he not been this through centuries? He has given penitence a voice; he gave our aspiration wings of prayer; he gave to gratitude a song of praise. David is as romantic a figure as ever stepped upon the stage of history—shepherd, warrior, musician, poet, statesman, conqueror, king. Myths meet in him, so rare a trysting-place he seems. A prodigious reason, a fertile imagination, a failing but recovering virtue, a great heart, a generous forgiveness, a thrilling eloquence, a genius for conquest, and an upleap of life toward God like spout of fountains,—this is David. And in "Saul" he dreams. The very spirit of poetry uses him as he his harp. He dedicates him to the cure of Saul. Man never is so great as when he serves; and young David is lost in service. Conquest loves him now as afterward; and Saul is roused into kingly life, consciousness, and action. The Jew's service to all races is herein set forth by symbol. All souls are debtor to the Jew. His Elijahs and Isaiahs, his Johns and Christ, have brought soul back to itself again. The greater David, Jesus, has done for all what David did for Saul. He hath brought us back to life—and God!

Lessing's "Nathan the Wise," written to inculcate catholicity, is noble and un-Jewish. He is figured as man first, Jew afterwards; while his race is Jew first, man afterwards. Lessing's fable of the three rings is sophistical. An element of truth truly is contained. Dogmatism ought not to number us among its votaries. But truth is still truth. All systems are not equally true nor worthy of reception. Truth is one. Character may be catholic in treatment, but must be intolerant of error. But in greatness of heart, Nathan is true to Jewry. Saul of Tarsus is not nobler than Nathan the Wise.

Shylock, in "Merchant of Venice," is no caricature. Browning's "Holy-cross Day" presents the Jew in a state of subordination; Shakespeare, in Shylock, presents the Jew with power, and using it—the Jew as aggressor. No one doubts that Abraham's sons can hate, or that they love money, and are adepts in procuring it. Shylock is true Jew. Commanding in ability, full of craft and finesse, unforgetting of injury, relentless in hate,—that is Shylock. The Jew has never lacked genius. By persecution, a race once rooted to the soil like Lebanon's cedars, has become wanderer and exile. His occupation as portable merchantman has been thrust upon him. He must have wealth transportable to new shores, else penury would be his portion. This is the genesis of the Jew as clothier, jeweler, broker. To-day here, to-morrow yonder; to-day a confidant of kings and cabinets, to-morrow harried from the realm like noisome pestilence; but he has been genius wherever thrown. He has not lacked sagacity. In spite of shipwrecks of fortune so multitudinous as to baffle enumeration or conjecture, his fleets still sailed the seas. Shylock was penurious. He and gold were lovers. But the nobler of ignoble vices masters him. Hate conquers miserliness. This man who has ridiculed and despised him is now in his power, and no man shall save him. Yellow ducats shall not dull the edge of hate. Shout in his ears, "Take four times the bond's face," and he will not hear you for exulting in his knife, hungry for blood. He is a Jew, and hates the Christian dog. Race, bigotry, misuse, all appeal to him, and not in vain. "Vengeance! Vengeance!" Shylock, though a Jew at a disadvantage, is still Jew in lineament, vernacular, trait, conduct.

Isaac, in "Ivanhoe," is one face of Shylock; he loves his daughter and his gold. The rack shall not wring from him the hiding-place of his wealth. He protests, makes appeal to Abraham's God to attest his poverty, declares he has been robbed of all his gold by insatiable John, a story not at all incredible; but Rebecca is above gold. What no rack can torture from him, fear for his Rebecca extracts with swift immediacy. Isaac is not admirable, but is yet not devoid of attractions. His cringing speech we can ill tolerate; but the love of his widowed heart for his Rebecca is beautiful. The Jew is much a lover. Jacob serving for Rachel, and accounting his seven years brief as a winter's day for the love he bore her, is an idyl perennially beautiful as half-blown roses. Whoever studies the Jew in history or in flesh, must be touched by his affection. Fidelity is an attribute of his character. Rebecca, sad, tearless, fair, sad with the pathos of unrequited love, is not fiction. She is true Jewess. Womanhood goes far to find truer interpretation of womanliness than the Jewess gives. Home instinct, which is heart instinct, is an Israelitish virtue. Only the Anglo-Saxon has approximated them in this. Not Roman nor Greek knew like fidelity. For centuries of ancient time the Jew had the sole *home* among the races; and considering how absolutely essential experience has demonstrated the home to be to civilization, the Jew's major part in its establishment should never be forgotten. Isaac was father and mother to Rebecca, as Simonides to Esther; and he loved her above his gold. She was his chief joy, and in her was a purity, a quiet self-poise, a hid might of love, a capacity for suffering and for secret-keeping which glorify all womanhood, and are innate in Jewish character.

To "Hypatia" we are indebted for two graphic delineations—mother and son, Miriam and Raphael Aben-Ezra. Miriam is a woman in whom all womanliness is dead save mother-love, and minds us of Fantine in "Les Miserables." She is apostate to her faith, fallen, vile, procuress, an adept in craft, has a Midas touch which turns all she touches into gold, is one ubiquitous incognito, holds the secrets of lives and cabinets, seems aimless as a dismantled ship; though, in fact, led of one consuming passion,—she loves her son, who knows not he has a mother. She watches him as guardian angels do. She fills his hands with wealth, as if he were son of a Cæsar. She withholds nought save only knowledge of herself. At last she dies for him; and in that death with the white face of her and the great love of her, fallen, but a woman yet with heart deeper than deep seas, these seem half expiation of her guilt. Nor is she all un-Jewish. That Jews have become apostate and conjurer is an oft-told story. Baseness is a possible application of might. Miriam was great in her fall. Raphael, as first seen, is fop, gambler, spendthrift; or so he seems. He impresses us as being weak as rushes swinging beside summer streams, toys of every wind. But his is assumed frivolity. He wears it as a mask. He is no fiction. History has produced characters not a few who disguised depth under apparent superficiality. Raphael's mind has compass, and he is possessed of both brain and worth, and was not the shallow, babbling stream we thought him. Heroisms, mastery of philosophies, acceptance of the Christ, were latent in him. And he adds one more to the list of Jewish strength in fiction, and one more to the roll of those whose awakening to the better gives life renewed hope.

Zangwill, in "The Children of the Ghetto," concerns himself mainly with the lower strata of Jewry; and Jewry, like humanity, has its lower as its upper. There is no reason to doubt the veracity of this novel. The symptoms are certainly Jewish. The peripatetic poverty; the man with a memory of love and joy, but no present manhood or power apparent of making a home for homeless children; his son, sprung out of this shiftlessness, rising to the point of being scholar and more, when death called him and he went; his daughter, gifted with grace of fancy and facility of pen, bearing ostracism stoically as no old Greek knew to do, revealing the secret of the real Jew's condition, finding at last, as a tossed ship after wild storms, a haven of perpetual love,— this we are told in realistic fashion as we are shown the ordinary, unengaging life of a Ghetto, whether at London or at Rome. The fish smells and shrewd bargaining, the quaint customs and love-makings, the petty horizons for the many lives, the cheer and gladness inseparable from life, the exact ritualism not lessened since Pharisee of old made broad his phylactery, and lengthened prayers, and observed jots and tittles of ceremonial law or meaningless formularies,—all this is set down with minute fidelity and graphic portrayal. The rabbi who could watch with unchanged face the breaking of his daughter's heart, but would adhere to immemorial forms at so great a hazard, aspiration refusing to die, but finding in Jewry no sufficient goal,—these seem the logical and coherent utterances of one who knew. This nether world is a Jew's world still, for poverty does not expatriate. Fraternity knits Hebrews together with threads of steel. They keep a solid front to the world. The "Children of the Ghetto" gives views not afforded by any other fiction; and what we care to know is truth, the entire truth. Who paints a portrait studies all moods of the subject. This complex character the Jew will compel many sittings and many attitudes, since he is so composite. Valleys are as natural to the world as mountains. All topographical features have their place. Deserts are real as fertile fields; and the Ghetto is real as Rothschild's princeliness. Filth, while no anticipation of the Mosaic code for this chosen people since Leviticus presents a perfect hygienic system—filth is yet a fact of Jewish memorabilia. All civilization has ghettoes, as has the Jew. Humanity must bear the imputation of being unclean in body, as in spirit. And in this Jew's Ghetto are hints of comedy and bits of tragedy, and boisterous merrymaking native to all estates. Poverty is no dethronement of delight. Heroisms, too, are here. Souls are the tenting-grounds of the heroic. No life is cut off from the possibility of nobleness; and the revelation of an old father, conscious that his presence jeopards his son's happiness; who feigns a brother in far-off America, who has sent for him to share his wealth, and so leaves this Ghetto, though to leave is like tearing out his living heart, and turns gray face toward an unknown land,—such sacrifice renews the courage of us all. Beyond dispute we are debtors to this guide, who has led us along so untrod, novel, and fascinating a path.

In Sue's "Wandering Jew" and Wallace's "Prince of India" the fact pertinent to this discussion is the longevity of the Jew—a perpetual wonder, whose coming brings a curse! For in this wanderer's shadow epidemics settle like baleful dew. He curses all he loves. Not health, but disease, is his contribution to his world. He can not die. No one can gainsay this to be a truth of Jewish history. In the "Prince of India" the immortal Jew is malignant; in "The Wandering Jew" he is beneficent. The Jew is both. Far-reaching in plans, power of accomplishment, perpetual wandering as if our earth were one unbroken Sinai wilderness, a life-long hunger at the heart, an inability to die,—are these not accurate as if they were history rather than fiction?

The "Scape-goat" gives Israel Ben Olliel,

than whom no more pathetic portrait of the Jew has been painted. He repeats his race in intellect, in a strong and unflinching sense of God, in ability to live within himself, in love for wife and daughter, in mastery of men, in invincibility of spirit when once his conscience is let lead, in his dignity which defies humiliation. Israel Ben Olliel compels your veneration, admiration, love; and you can readily believe of him his biographer's statement that his was the noblest head he had seen set on man's shoulders. He was a son of David, born to rule. Even a cruel and vicious ruler became palatable in part when his counsels were directed by this astute minister. He knew to suffer; his loneliness is pitiful. His wife drifts from him like some boat borne away by the current of a stream. His little daughter, blind, deaf, dumb, breaking by littles through all these barriers to a command of every faculty; the biting hatred of the synagogue heaping contumely upon him, a whole people cursing a man who was in truth their best friend; disgrace at his master's hands when he became non-compliant; bereft of power, nothing shelters him from mob violence and prison sequestration; but in every place looking the what he was, a mighty spirit habituated to self-control so complete as to let no perturbation fling shadow across his face, his ability to inspire fidelity and love in those who knew him best, so that brave "Ali died with his name upon his lips, and with a dauntless shout of triumph," his love of Naomi the beloved, in whom after God his life was set as in a garden,—this is Israel Ben Olliel; and both man and face may well arrest us. "It is a big, strong face with a snow-white beard. His hair, too, is long and white. A Jovian head, and a face with some of the grander lines of the ancient and heroic race of Israel." He is sitting in squalor at his poor mud-hut door, bare of foot and head, with worn garment, wandering eyes, bearded chin bowed on his clenched hands, as if snow had slipped from the tent roof and had half hid them, so white and ample his beard, and talking to himself in the English tongue; "and he was mumbling terms of endearment, coupled sometimes with a name;" for he was daughterless. She has been seized by his sometime prince as an addition to his seraglio. So love lives on when mind lies dead. And now dying, Naomi holding his dear head upon her breast, singing to him,

> "Love, great love,
> O come and claim thine own,
> O come and take thy throne,
> Reign ever and alone,
> Reign, glorious, golden love,"—

while Israel Ben Olliel makes shift to beat time for her singing, looking love, love only, life's day forgotten—it is evening now—whispering, "Never was she so dear to me as now. Remember, remember!" "Listen! When I am there, eh?—you know *there*—I will want to say, Father, you did well to hear my prayer. My little daughter—she is happy," and murmuring with last articulate word, "God—is—great," and taking hand of lover and bringing it to his breast, where lay Naomi's hand "beneath his own trembling one," and "with that last effort, and a look into Naomi's face that must have pursued him home, his grand eyes closed forever." Him lying white and still there, say with the Mahdi, "He has gone *to the King!*" One is not often moved as by that gray face and noble head.

"Daniel Deronda" is a study of the Jew

from unexpected quarters. George Eliot was agnostic. To her, "the oracles of God" were mythic voices. God in history, Gentile or Jewish, was never more than suspected; could never be assured, since God was a question-mark. The Jew comes to be of absorbing interest only in the light of his theistic history. Hebrews, descendants of Abraham, are of interest; Hebrews, the chosen of God, whose history is punctuated with miracle, are of absorbing interest. George Eliot, entertaining nugatory theories of Hebrew history, was yet, as a woman of imagination and heart, caught in the meshes of this stranger romance than Sindbad had ever attempted telling. She was probably more impressed by the miraculous than herself knew. In any case, she has given us a latter-day study of a Jew, thrilled with enthusiasm for Hebrew history and the morrow of his race; and Mordecai is a character who might have stood in his ranks in the schools of the prophets. Every Jew's character in "Daniel Deronda" is individual, and logical in conception, and apt to its purpose. Deronda's mother is typical, and more than possible. She was restless under the Jewish ban, was defective in imagination as in devotion in love. Hebrew past held no glory to light the present. She repudiated her race, and all but repudiated her son. No question the countess has sisters among her people. The Jew sits solitary and apart, as he were an oblation to the gods. This she could not brook. No doubt but that in this isolation is something drastic to many women. If we may interpret the utterances of the recent Convention of Jewesses, they and the countess are of one mind. They resist restriction to race marriages. They feel hindered as birds meant for woods, but shut in cages. Love brooks no hindrances, but cares to walk free as the moon across the world. Deronda's mother represents a recalcitrancy in the Jewish heart, this is clear. How widely spread this feeling, is not pertinent to the discussion. That it exists, is justification for our author's character. But we can not be pleased with this countess. She has practically deserted her son, who through years supposed himself dishonored in his birth. Deronda's meeting with his mother was frigid, and entirely lacking in that plethora of maternal tenderness characterizing the Jewess. In any race, however, are abnormalities. Woman is meant for and attains ideality, but, falling, falls so low that none but Christ would attempt her restoration. The Cohens are well portrayed. He is the vender, the cunning, busy money-getter, and lover of store-shelves and little Jacob and his devoted admirer. I have been on shipboard with such Jewish families as the Cohens; and the sight of them did one good, that lingers in memory a blessing still. Cohen is real, more real than Mordecai, because the matter-of-fact man is the multitudinous man. He fills each census table full; but the common man is man, tender, heroic on occasion, bearing marks of being God's son. Cohen is true to his race, true to every race.

Then the Anathoths, father, son, daughter. Mirah is least racial of the three. Man, as lover, loses his race qualities. Love obliterates race distinctions, and has one attitude and one speech. Jessica and Mirah and Ophelia alike repeat in whispers to their own hearts in darkness, "I love him, I love him." Love flings us out of the tribal into the universal. The larger instincts of soul are world instincts. At every step we transcend both place and clan. The father is baseness, naming himself a Jew. Not often have we looked on so degraded a man, nor one so lost to virtue. The father of Robert Falconer, as drawn by MacDonald, is not so fallen as this man. Anathoth has deserted his children, leaving them to die or survive as they might; but when once they come to positions where he may spoil them, he appears. He is a leech. His food is blood, nor is he choice whose blood it is. He will not be sybarite, only give him blood. He is cringing as Uriah Heep, and finds son and daughter, but to disgrace them as a common thief. Yet he shames not them so much as us. All men are shamed in one man's sin. It reflects evil hues on every face. To fall so low as to lose sense of shame, to see a face flushed with love as Mirah's is, and not enter into compact for her happiness, to see Mordecai and signs of dissolution on him, to know a fire burns this husk to a last flaring flame, to be sure you look a modern prophet in the face, and not awake to manhood,—is too pitiful for words. Yet with such a sire, woman could be pure of heart, and man could dwell in a celestial sphere wrapt round with clouds of purple and of gold. Mordecai was son of such a sire. He is drawn a prophet and a poet. He was a flame leaping toward heaven. As Hegel was absorbed in his philosophy, Mordecai was absorbed in his prophetic dreams. Deronda's mother thought to be Hebrew a calamity; Mordecai thought it to be the sum of blessings. Israel was God's chosen among all races. the Benjamin whom God held exceeding dear. Mordecai was enthusiast, was possessed by noble dreams. Such as he Isaiah was: That flushed face of genius; those eyes which see through darkness as through light; the voice in which are cadences of exquisite music; that hand, whose touch, as Kingslake in "Eothen" says, "Crept like a whisper up the listening palm;" that sincere, clean, rapt soul, which in the world dwelt in forgotten zones of thought and inspiration. Mordecai is the Jew as dreamer. He might have been musician, painter, orator, poet. Who could put Mordecai on canvas, could paint Ezekiel when beside the river Chebar he "saw visions of God."

But Daniel Deronda is the Jew as modern gentleman, and is altogether admirable. No blemish scars his character. Even when he sets sail upon a fatuous voyage, we can not wish him other than he was. Innumerable things are worse than being Don Quixote; for he was an idealist and a gentleman. Scholar, man of leisure, modest, pure as air that haunts high mountains, strong enough to have strength to be a strength to Gwendolyn Harleth and a fulfillment to Mordecai, imaginative enough to dream, the Orient flushing his cheek, the Occident girding his purpose, steady in movement, reserve of power his possession, Deronda moves like a brave ship which walks billows as if they were a meadowland. He is Jew of the highest type; but his ancestry is unknown. George Eliot has evidenced superior art in disclosing hidden movements of spirit, which become explicable only when race ancestry is discovered. This Jewish ancestry has not more flushed his cheek than it has colored his mentality and character. Radiant eastern nights seem flooding his soul with spendthrift glory. Finding who he is, he understands himself. Mordecai wakes him as if Deronda were instrument and Mordecai musician. This Jew, a great past seizes, and holds him prisoner; and then he dreams that yesterdays imply to-morrows. Capable of enthusiasm as large life must be, Daniel Deronda is a praise to the race whose product he is assumed to be.

And "Ben Hur,"—with him ends this procession of fiction. Princess Hur, Tirzah, Esther, Simonides, Ben Hur,—surely we have watched a royal procession pass! Israel is in the book,—Israel's pomp, disaster, fidelity in love, wealth of tenderness, brilliancy of achievement, unbreakable will, race instinct, the ruddy life outliving tragedy expectant for another day, defeated, triumphant; such is Ben Hur, such is Israel.

Esther is sweet daughter, worthy her tender and heroic sire,—strong, delicate in love as woman in her finer moments is, she breaks on the spirit as moonrise; Tirzah, sister to Ben Hur, prisoner, leprous, forgotten, discovered, healed of Christ; Princess Hur, pitiful in her woes, but upborne by faith in God. "By the rivers of Babylon we sat down and wept, yea, we wept when we remembered Zion;" but she a prisoner on Zion's hill, and saw no sunrise smite the golden roof of Jehovah's temple! This tragedy of imprisonment is typical tyranny, relentless, terrible. A leper, yet drinking at the deep fountains of love, she dreams of Ben Hur, hopes for him, prays God for him. Her hope lives on. Ben Hur runs like a living stream through the parched desert of her life.

With woman's wondrous decentralization of soul, she slurs her own wrong and suffering over thinking of Tirzah, more of Ben Hur. She saw him last lost in the procession moving toward the galleys. Hear her cry, "Ben Hur! Ben Hur! Ben Hur!" And love has always one recourse, love. She was not all bereft. Tirzah and her love and God did keep her company. Not often has any writer given so pathetic a picture as that of Tirzah and the Princess Hur stealing like shadows of the night down from En Rogel's well to look by night upon the home of their remembered joy. And Ben Hur lies sleeping on the step of Prince Hur's palace, across whose wide doors even eyes dimmed with leprosy can read written, "This is the property of the emperor." Ben Hur turns him restless in his dreams, and moans, "Mother." And Princess Hur sees him for whom all these dead years she has longed as dying lips for the dear kiss of love. Tirzah sees his hand lying palm upward, and will pour kisses in its hollow like rain into a rock; but the mother withholds with strident leprous whisper, "Not for thy life, Leper!" She falls in the dust. A step, a word, a touch, a caress, a kiss, which had meant heaven; but she whispers with her hoarse sibilant of leper's speech, "Unclean, unclean!" And this sweet, self-denying life creeps, only to press parched lips to his dusty sandal sole—and creeps back, a shadow among shadows. How high love soars what time her wings are spread! But in Amrah with her deep fidelity, in Esther, the princess, and Tirzah, aside from their persistency and beauty of love, Jewry finds no articulate speech.

Simonides and Ben Hur are the Jewish spirits. Simonides is majestic. All we learn of him—and we know him from a lad—is to his praise. He knew how to love with a great and tender passion, such as moved Jacob to serve a slave for Rachel. For love he became a slave forever. That was love! His paternal affection was sweet as odors of lilacs. He might have ruled a Roman empire. His was a faithfulness which knew no sleeping nor abatement of toil through many years, when hope of his master's return must have died on many days like crimson from evening clouds—his glad surrender of the colossal fortune which his genius for trade had amassed, and with it listing himself and Tirzah as chattels of Prince Hur! Cupidity slinks away ashamed in Simonides' presence. Look at him—his princely brow, his commanding intellect, his vast mastery of the currents of trade, his riches exceeding those of the Cæsars even. We thought this fiction? 'T is history rather. It is from Rothschild kings must borrow in their hour of need. In Nathan the Wise, Israel Ben Olliel, and Simonides, find Jewish captivity, character, and genius. But consider Simonides' moral fiber beyond what we have already seen. He is wheeled to and fro—you notice that. Some wreck has crushed him. Nay, that wreck was Gratus, who, having confiscated Prince Hur's palace and estate, hearing Simonides was Prince Hur's steward, broke him on the rack to make him disclose the hiding-place of his gold. The rack creaked, Simonides' face grew white, his muscles lengthened, his arms tore from the sockets, his tendons crack like strings on a musician's instrument—"Tell now, tell now," this it is Gratus says; and Simonides, white now as in death, faints; is taken from the rack a shapeless mass of bones and flesh, to be wheeled to and fro as children are, but his lips are sealed—and he keeps his secret! That is Simonides, and he is an honor to our race.

And this is Ben Hur beside him. Recite his history, and you seem rehearsing Israel's story. A prince of David's house, loved, opulent, he is hurried to galley slavery. Chained, he tugs at the oars; is bent, and not broken. He knits thews like Nimrod's as he plies his oar. Upon a battle-day with pirates, his chain is loosed; he joins the battle, is flung from the wrecked galley, rescues Arrius the duumvir, is adopted as his son and heir, is schooled at the Roman ludi and academe; but not for an hour does he forget mother, Tirzah, Jerusalem. They haunt him, as shadows do the hills. He owes a debt; he will be true. He seeks in vain; the waves of years have washed their very footprints from the shore; they are but memories. But at Antioch, capital of Syria, at the circus, he meets the author of his disaster, Messala, rich, haughty, imperious; a Roman, therefore cruel. Ben Hur is Jew, and knows how to hate, as he knows how to love. He has sheikh Ilderim's eagles from the desert, and plans to be avenged through them. The Roman circus, the procession of competitors, the exact maneuver, the iron muscles, the self-mastery written on his face, the imperturbable rocking in the reeling chariot, persistency of purpose cruel as the grave, the crash, Messala wounded for life, and the race won! Is not that the Jew? You must love Ben Hur. His youth, his suffering, his unbroken spirit, his constancy of filial love, his resistance in Daphne's grove, his physical might, his vast composure, his settled purpose, his love for Esther, and his final love for Christ,—you must love Ben Hur.

And this pageant is all passed. We hear not footfalls, but echoes; and now, when the procession is vanished, say: "We have seen a prince among races pass." These Jews thrill us as the Romans did not. They mystify us like a prophecy. Their achievements and history, their prowess and capacity, their love and devotion, their sense of God at hand, their unbewildered hope, their fortitude and heroism and disaster and services to mankind,—all break across the spirit like some driving sea; and we are as those bewildered by the shock.

Robert Burns

POETRY, in common with other utterance, is exponential. Men speak from the heart. In instances not a few, this exponential character is so pronounced that the poetry becomes autobiographical. This was the case with Byron, as it was with Shelley. We seem to be reading confessions as certainly as when we read Rousseau or Goethe. In Shakespeare's dramas, however, personality is absolutely wanting. He is impersonal. We can not reconstruct this colossus from his plays; for, like his players, he wears a mask. Of no poet do we know so little, because his speech does not betray him. Even in his sonnets, there is but dubious light thrown on the face of this poet laureate of the world. In "Paradise Lost" we get scarcely a clue to guide us through the maze of the Miltonic life. In Robert Browning the traces of self-revelation are as uncertain as a footpath through a woodland in the dark.

But this Scottish lyrist, Robert Burns, is as communicative as a child. He is no sphinx to keep secrets hid behind a stony brow. The tell-tale blushes on a woman's cheek are not more self-revealing than the poetry of this rare son of tarn and fell, burn and crag, of loch and ben. I think it quite within bounds of truth to say we learn more of Burns from his poems than from his letters. The letters are stilted, artificial, scarcely sincere, certainly far from natural. In them he is in dress-suit, and is self-conscious. It is, however, as if in all his verse he had said, "I will tell you one thing more about myself." With this flavor on all Burns has written, his poetry becomes picturesque as the explanatory clause of a strange life in which the whole world is come to have an interest. His poetry is himself, and himself is Scotland. This I take to be one cause of the perennial popularity of his writings. Since those leaves were blown as by autumn's blast from Scotland's trees, the interest in their beauty has abated not a whit. Men read them now with the same pathetic thought as when the fate of Burns was a fresh memory to the heart.

Burns is the common people's poet. Charles Dickens was himself when he described middle class or slum life of that England whose social historian he was. Outside of such circle his movement is uncertain as a bird lost in the drift of storm. Burns was and is to Scotland what Dickens is to England, with this reservation, that he attempted the one thing his genius was suited to, as music to poet's words. He knew his limitations, nor attempted to pass them. But Burns was more than a singer for Scotland. He speaks for the common man. This is the meaning of his dialect; for Burns is the greatest writer of dialect. Out of this he was never at home. He has immortalized a strange, sweet speech. How the Scotch tongue abounds in beautiful diminutives! The "wee bit, cowerin', timorous beastie" could not have been written in English. The verse is absolutely indigenous to Scotland. You can not transplant it. Burns is untranslatable. He belongs, and must belong, to the land of his nativity, as entirely as the laverock or his mountain daisy. He spoke the people's speech. This is the potent secret of the growing audiences this poet's minstrelsy gathers. We common men people the world. The land is ours; and we must have a voice. Dialect is the language of the common folk. Travel, culture, society, wear away provincialism in speech by their attrition. Culture tends to make a universal language. But the common man is, in a sense, planted in the soil. He belongs to a locality; and thought and speech are flavored by this environment; and to hear a poet use common men's language is to feel him brother. Of Burns, a world will exclaim, "He sings for us; this is our poet, singing songs we could not articulate." Burns is not visitor in his world; he is inhabitant. He does not look and speak; he lives and speaks. For the toil to which most men find themselves heirs, he stops to sing. The plow stands still mid-furrow while the Mousie is a-writing, or while the Daisy is having her elegy written. The world wants a spokesman; and Burns is he. And our spokesman shall be dear to us, as son to father. Popularity arises from this fact, as may readily be seen. He is the voice of common man, and our voice shall not be permitted to echo itself into silence. This is the very fortress of Burns's strength. He is knit into dialect. Out of it he was another and a lesser man. He was no figure for the palace halls—Tennyson was that—but belonged to the field and its dewy morning. He seems a piece of nature. He and the daisy are alike indigenous to the soil. Toil speaks in him. His were the songs of labor and the songs of love. Toil singing, that is Burns. And labor ought to sing. Toil is not morose, but full of singing and laughter, and calls, "My poet, sing for me."

Burns has given Scotland an immortal voice. In a later day, Scott, with wizard touch, opened wide the book of Scotch history, locality, and character. But to history and geography Burns gave little heed, and to character —Scotland's character, Burns's character— he gave all heed. We go to Scotland to-day because Burns and Scott have put the passion in the blood. You will note the difference between the method of these two. Scott makes history and topography chief. He puts emphasis on castle, rock, and glen. Burns never does. These, if they appear in his poetry, are there as unconsciously as the rare flavor of Scotch dialect. History he is not alive to. Experience is all, the setting as it may be; since Burns is where he is, it could be no other. But we must always feel he is not writing about Scotland; he is spokesman for his race and common man. He tells their story, and takes us into the confidence of a strange, attractive, and profound clan among earth's peoples. The world has not lost interest in Scotland since Burns spoke for it. Its voices have been in our ears, like the sound of far-off waters heard at night. A fascination has clung about kirk and cottage, which abides like the heather on the moors. Scotch character is unique. Taciturn, undemonstrative, unostentatious, seemingly hard, a handshake instead of a kiss, actually leal as morning to the sun, unspeakably tender, self-respecting, a humor indulging in no laughter, but cutting deep; loyal to Scotland, fixed to localities, intense in localism, abstemious, forcing a livelihood from nature's niggardliness, high-idealed, intensely religious, a profound moral consciousness with its inevitable concomitant an alert conscience,—such, in poor outline, is Scotch character, and a study of perennial attractiveness. Dr. John Brown, Barrie, and Ian Maclaren may thank Robbie Burns for their constituency. The life this bard of poverty made so much of will be a theme whose interest will never flag. Nor is the land less attractive than the character rooted in its soil. The babble of runnels, the limpid pool, the highland loch, the dash of waterfalls, the dark mountain-side shaded with pines standing solemn and changeless,—these constitute a land of unusual beauty. History, climate, topography, character, all Scotch and all classic now; and Scott and Burns have made them so. Yet now that we think of it, Burns makes little of these accessories. He barely mentions the sea. How strange that is, and what a sense of loss is on us in the lack! Burns is no painter of landscapes. He is figure-painter. A face, his art means that. What scenery we have in him is inferential; but the life of Scotland, the lofty patriotism, his glory in manhood and assertions of equality, how these voices make the pulse throb!

There is in Burns, as an exponent of Scotch character, absolute fidelity, characteristic humor, somber simplicity, adherence to duty, a scorn of sham, strength, music, and heart,— these phrases are descriptive of the salient features of his poetry. His pictures are true. "The Cotter's Saturday Night" illustrates two qualities of Burns, his accuracy of delineation and the somber hues of Scotch thought and action. One sees the scene, not because he tries, but because he can not help it. The measured methodicality of the Scot is seen in what was done, and in the order of the doing. Can future Scotland fail to know eighteenth century Scotland after this poem has given the picture? A stenographer's report had not been more accurate. The flavor of duty, the going the way ordained, is always inseparable from a noble Scotch life. Fealty to duty is the largest quality of soul, and no people has ever known the art of burning this principle on the heart more indelibly than the Scotch. Their literature is filled with it. Harsh this code of conduct may be, but heroic it always is. It glorifies men and women, and they seem walking in this as in a sunset. The exceeding beauty of the Highland Marys lies in their simplicity, fidelity, and purposeful existence.

Scotch humor is all but unequaled. There is in it a touch of acid; but rare humor it is. Tam O'Shanter—what could be more native, accurate, and grave? Gravity is always an element in this Scotch humor. One can imagine the great delight with which a coterie of tavern worthies would rehearse this tale as they sat around their cups. "To a Louse on a Lady's Bonnet" seems to me captivating. He who can refrain from laughter in reading this bit of jocularity, surely has no humor in himself, and is fit for one knows not what. The "Address to the Deil" is a bit of humor which fairly inebriates. Burns evidently saw the fun of things, and, in that sober Scotch way which eschews laughter, throws auditors into convulsions.

But humor can never constitute a man a poet. Love, duty, and pathos are materials of poetry. In the noblest verse, as in Tennyson, the element of sadness is omnipresent. Tears, not laughter, are in the poet's eyes. We can lose Burns's bacchanals and feel no loss, but his hymns of the heart we can not do without. Bannockburn! Why, it clashes like Miriam's cymbals! Our blood boils like the sea in tempest. The fervor of heroic days thunders in our ears the call to war. No nobler ode to liberty has been written.

Burns was erratic, fickle, false, restive, intemperate, melancholy, and moody as a Scotch sky. His fits seize him. He was a creature of moments. Laughter or weeping, no one could tell which should proceed from this minstrel. A big heart, a feverish passion, a lust for wine and women, a manhood burned out like a candle to the socket,—this is Burns. He was a man with his full share of weakness and wickedness, but with a large endowment of genius, nobility, and vision; and we pass his aberrancies by tenderly, because of the manhood he did possess. With Burns the world has forgotten much. His was a trumpet for freedom. That there was, however, something of belligerency in his notions of equality and freedom, we can not in truth deny. He was in fierce unrest with his condition. Contentment he no more knew than do caged eagles. He saw clearly that a man was a man for his own sake and in his own name; that blood was not to be tested by age, but by quality. But he rebelled against being poor. He did not feel safe within himself in conscious dignity. He therefore railed at those above him. Calm, dispassionate, he never was. He did not know how to be unperturbed as fate. What scion of a noble house in this era whose fame is comparable with the fame of Burns? Why did he not rest his dignity on his worth? He was not thus. Fever was on him. Passion burned on his pages, and made his poems invectives. But aside from this blemish, there is in him vision of man as man and worth as worth, which much of a commonplace as it is with us when America has familiarized the earth with this idea, was in the eighteenth century seen dimly when at all.

Burns's poetry is essential music. Verse may be either the poetry of music or the poetry of thought. Some poets contribute thought to the soul. They must enlarge the mind to contain the thoughts they bring. They are vessels laden with merchandise, piled in hold and high upon the deck. To be a wharf at which such ships unlade is to enlarge the soul till it becomes ample as the shore of ocean. Shakespeare will do this. You must become philosopher if you stay in his company. With him, music is subordinate to logic. Arguments march like battle-ranks. He will have you see souls struggle as wrestlers in the Olympic games. You grow fatigued like a traveler climbing steep and long ascents. So with Browning; you may not play but must labor, if you are to be his companion. Weighty truths startle your spirit. Music is secondary. The inspiration is the massiveness of thought. Cyclops lifts for you. Other poets are poets of music. They sing. Their thought is of minor consequence, and would not bear analysis. Yet what thought has the singing lark? You do not ask that, because the singing suffices. And this is the true estimate; poets of thought and poets of music are not enemies, but friends. Each has his ministry, and his ministry is his apology. Music is an end. Burns is not a thought poet. He has not given one new thought or a vigorous idea. Nor is this a discourtesy to say of him; for he was not a thinker, that is all; but he was a singer. Music has power of its own, nor does it need to borrow thought, since it *is* thought. Music makes you dream. Who, having listened to noble melody (with closed eyes as is best), but has found his soul in a state of ferment ere the music sobbed into silence? Vast unrest seized him. He felt himself capable of the heroic. He was an unfettered might. Music had loosed him and let him go. Do we not see how aspiration is its own justification? How that is life's chief desideratum, and therefore how ample a vindication the poet of music has? His music lifts us as mountains do not; and Burns is a musician.

His genius was lyric, not didactic nor epic. Those who hold Burns might have written a national epic, seem to me to obscure the main truths of his literary character. "The Cotter's

Saturday Night" is not Burns at his best, though the contribution is one we would not willingly let die. As of old the troubadour sung to the music of the harp, and melody of hand and lip rose together, so this poet's verse is of the lyre. It was meant for singing. It sings itself. You can no more keep Burns's words from music, than you can keep the wimple from singing in the glen.

His poetry is essential music. Like streams among his native crags, his poems ripple with laughter and delight. Strange melodies are nurtured among those Northern hills. Who that has heard a bagpipe play can well forget its haunting music? And many of Burns's poems were written to fit Scottish airs. They were fitted to music. If ever a purely lyric poet lived and wrote, Burns was that poet. I doubt not his poems sang themselves in his mind. Redundant with love and hope, sick with despair, bugle-note of triumph, philippic against the existing order, whatever theme, whatever temper, music was never wanting. A skylark singing toward the sky in the first flush of morning has not sweeter notes than this child of the Scotch glen.

But Burns's heart was his noblest potency.

Because his music bubbles from the heart as water from hidden springs, we can not elude its witchery. Logic we may be deaf to; but one language is universal speech; namely, the language of the heart. When his heart speaks, it is that Burns becomes dynamic. He changes love often; but his love speaks passion at the hour. Love must always have lute and voice. It is the master inspiration of the world. And as long as love lives (and who does not know love to be immortal as the heart?) Burns will be her minstrel. We forget his constancy lasted but a day in the fervor of his protestations of undying affection. With him love seems as love always should, fresh as dew on flowers of morning. To love is to see but her, hear but her. The lovers straying across hills scented with heather-bloom, or down the burn where the waters themselves seem whispering like lovers the oft-repeated story; the parting mixed of kisses and of tears; the praying for the coming of evening star when lips shall meet once more,—these are pictures whose colors are unfading so long as Burns shall sing love lyrics in our ears. Himself has said, that with him love and poetry awoke together. The sonsie highland lassie was inspirer of his poet's song. Love has ever a singing heart; and who that has heard song of a woman looking for her lover must know love has singing lips. Love is tender, and caresses its native speech. Burns is filled with tenderness. Tears keep watch in his eyes. "The Daisy," "To a Mouse," "On Seeing a Wounded Hare Limp by Me," are all utterances of the heart not less certainly than his songs of love. Susceptible to every fair face, he was not less so to every inspiration. His moods were changing as moods of sky. Tears chase laughter from his face as drink drove reason from his brain. But love of nobleness was in him; and the passionate gift of song used him as if he had been a lute. Love of truth, country, river, cushat, mousie, daisy, lassie (be she Mary, Eliza, or Jean),—that was Burns's literary biography. Love means melancholy; and it is quite beyond credence how persistently shadows hang over all Burns wrote, until you take his poems and go over them at a sitting. Rollicking he seems to be, but sad at heart you will always find him. The fear of parting is on his meeting with Mary. "The Daisy" is rich in this sentiment, which thrills all his poetry. Every poet is impressionable. He runs to catch the form of things. And as sandstone holds prints of waves which long ago ran up the strand of some forgotten sea, so in this poet's songs we trace the play of variant and vagrant moods. And as in voices of the laughing tide, there still remain reminiscences of storms and tales of shipwreck, in Burns is whisper of

"And forward though I canna see, I guess and fear."

> "Even thou who mourn'st the daisy's fate,
> That fate is thine—no distant date;
> Stern ruin's plowshare drives, elate
>   Full on thy bloom;
> Till crushed beneath the furrow's weight
>   Shall be thy doom."

The Psychology of Nathaniel Hawthorne

HAWTHORNE looked a genius and a gentleman. And his face did neither misconceive nor misrepresent him. Genius does not always, nor even as a rule, communicate itself to the features. Many a mediocre looks a sage, and many a sage looks a mediocre. Mind does not undertake to show its credentials. The kingdom of intellectuality is a hid kingdom. In rare instances, however, mind and body conspire together; and a man looks the thing he is. Bearing, poise of head, secret-revealing eyes, mobile features, noble brow, sensitive mouth,—these with mute eloquence assert, "Genius is come." Nathaniel Hawthorne falls into this company. Looking at his portrait, you would anticipate surprising powers, and be disappointed if he possessed them not. But Hawthorne will not disappoint you. He is America's representative man of letters.

Compare the faces of Hawthorne and Poe. There is a pronounced similarity. Look at them. Both speak the possession of genius. Both have sensitive faces, and both are sensitive men—Poe with coal-black hair, and eyes which fairly stabbed the air; Hawthorne with ruddy locks and quiet eyes. But both men saw. Both looked behind things. Both dealt with the unusual. They saw no ordinary sights. The thought of both was weird. One saw "The City in the Sea;" the other "Septimius Felton." Scan these faces closely. They are alike. No, they are unlike; and both observations are accurate. Similar they are, and dissimilar they are. Between the two is a great gulf. Poe's was a powerful genius, but it was sensuous. His is a body expression. His tales are terrible and harrowing as Stevenson or Hall Caine. He deals in machinery. His story moves madly like the maelstrom he depicts. Poe makes much of the external. He paints the visible. He could paint the torture of the damned, if canvas were afforded him. But Hawthorne stands solitary now. He and Poe have quit company, as travelers whose paths have parted. He makes little of the exoteric. His treatment of a theme is essentially spirituelle. The physical plays scant part on this stage. His theme is soul,

not body; his stage hidden, not apparent.
With Poe the tragic element is much, the
story is primary; with Hawthorne, the story
is slight, and there is little physical movement.
He is as the Fates, who weave in darkness.
Stand and watch a swollen river, whose turbulent current bears ice-drifts past you. You see
the sullen surface of the stream. It moves
visibly and swiftly toward the far-off, unseen
ocean; moves pitiless as an inquisitor. You
saw the riot of waters. Such is Poe's art.
But stand on the same bank when the river is
frozen over. You look across a field of snow
quiet as an Arctic night; no visible motion,
yet underneath, the waters, tireless, night and
day, push on toward the sea. We saw them
not, but they swept on. This is Hawthorne's
art.

Contrast the paintings of Munkacsy and
Hoffman. Munkacsy delights in many figures. In "Christ before Pilate" the Orient
seems gathered in the procurator's palace.
Two persons are central truly; but the many
are present. So in the recent picture, "Before
the Strike," the forms multiply like groups
of soldiery on eve of battle. He will construct
a background of faces. His canvas seems a

battle-piece, so crowded is it with figures. In Hoffman, on the contrary the figures are few at most; as in "Christ and the Young Ruler." He will throw the wealth of his skill into a single face, as he does in "Christ in Gethsemane." And Hawthorne is like Hoffman. He never multiplies figures. He is chary of characters. He is not as Dickens, who fairly bewilders with actors, who fills the stage, and whose creative power, productive as spring, grows a wilderness. Not so Hawthorne. He is a literary solitary who craves few companions. Four is his select number. Judging from his productions, he was believer in the sacred quaternion. There are four characters in "The Blithedale Romance;" four in "The House of Seven Gables;" four in "Septimius Felton;" four in "Marble Faun;" four in "Scarlet Letter." He rivets our gaze on a small company. All his talent is sacred to the elaboration of these four characters; and he brings them out in perpetual relief, as if he had scultpured them against a sky.

And Hawthorne is locative. He does not transplant characters. They are rooted in the soil as cedars are. There is magic in emigration. The voyage thrills the spirit; and the hope beyond the voyage thrills it more. And the migratory spirit has played no insignificant part in romance. "The Virginians" live and love in two worlds. "King Noanette" shifts continents. "John Inglesant" passes lightly from England to Italy as swallows do. "The Bondman" transports Red Jason from Iceland to the Isle of Mona, and back again, to work out the tragedy and triumph of his career and character. "Evangeline" is a wanderer; and you shall trace her love down the long shore of ocean, and up the great river's bank, by ashes of camp-fire and site of vanished tent. Evangeline wanders like the moaning wind,

"That seeks for rest, and rest can never find;"

"For Faith and Freedom" crosses the ocean, and to the Old World's wrongs adds the New World's deliverance. The sobs of seas, the flap of sails, the rattle of the oars in the rowlocks, and new scenes and rush of unexpected emotions,—these are on us when the history changes lands. We are watchers at a ship's prow, expecting discovery. But Hawthorne stays at home like homesick age. He is no wanderer, but holds fast to locality. Find where his story begins, and you will need no one to tell you where it ends. He holds to place like a lover. Life and death will need no more room than the radius of a stone's-cast to make their revelations. Recalling that this novelist lived in a New World, where distances were great, where, in consequence, the intellectual invitation to peregrination was insidious, where the love of localities had not in the nature of the case seized on civilization—recalling this, the wonder of Hawthorne's art grows on us. Environment can no more account for literature than for character. Life is not made, but self-made. Hawthorne haunts New England like a ghost. It is a magnet to attract him. Puritan place and temper have cast a spell over him. He is weird as the tossing of tree-tops seen in gathering darkness; but his wanderings will not lead him far. The fascination which held Hester Prynne a prisoner in the house of her shame, held Hawthorne and his fictions to a solitary spot.

Hawthorne is intensely introspective. He is no story-teller in the ordinary sense. He could have been that. Such an imagination as he possessed could have invented new theaters for fiction; but he chose a different route to immortality. What a story-teller Scott was! How events trample on each other, like cavalry horses rushing to battle! What a story-teller Weyman is! We shall listen many years to hear more stirring and strengthening tales told us than "A Gentleman of France" and "Under the Red Robe." What a story-teller Doyle is, if you listen to his "White Company" and to "Micah Clarke!" To my mind "Micah Clarke" is one of the strong historical romances of the last decade. And what a story-teller Gilbert Parker is! Thanks to him always for "The Seats of the Mighty." "The Three Guardsmen?" Yes, we hear the galloping steeds and the music of sword-play as these valiant musketeers charge past us, unpent tempests. "The Prisoner of Zenda" is a royal specimen of the relator's art. Its dash, naiveté, heroism, love, loss, longing, fealty to duty, and stimulation to nobilities in him who reads,—these make a story thrilling as Lancelot's warfare. Hawthorne rode not in these lists. He made no attempt to do these things. He belonged not to the field, but to the cell. Psychology is his choice of theme. He comes to souls. He will not look at a pageant pass the door, but will stand at the door and look into the habitation. He will not let us report for the soul, but will compel the soul to report for itself. This purpose, it will be observed, transfers us into the domain of genius. Shakespeare is psychologist, and calls, "Tell me thy comedy;" or "Sob thy tragedy to me." And Hawthorne will introduce us to the tragedy of souls. With death as a part of the machinery of fiction he has slight patience. What has the death of Arthur Dimmesdale to offer us matched with his living death? The gibbet on which he bared his secret to the world was welcome to him as any ship that ever bore homesick traveler home.

And more, it is a diseased psychology you must study, if Hawthorne is to be your preceptor. He is not grewsome. No odor of the morgue is perceptible in his tales. Not a delirious life as Ulalume, but a diseased and not a healthy life is considered. As a physician, he diagnoses a case. These men and women you shall meet are not usual folk. We feel to fear lest we look at ghosts. The color on the cheek is a hectic flush. Mystery hangs about them as mists about the tall cliffs of the sea. When we sight Lady Macbeth walking in her sleep through the dark with lit candle and wide-open eyes, we know something is awry. Or if Hamlet's ghost rise from his grave, and stalk a specter of midnight on the cliffs that fringe the surly ocean, Bernardo the soldier, as Horatio the scholar, will guess buried Denmark hides some dread secret at his heart. But we are not more conscious of mystery here than in Hawthorne's dramas. We feel we stand on the porch of tragedy, and if the door were to be pushed open, some specter would thrust us back into the dark. These houses are all haunted. Our shadows frighten us. We walk in mystery as those who walk in mists. Fogs lift; but this tragic element never lifts its shadow from Hawthorne's page. The romance ended, the mystery is only deepened and mocks you like ghostly laughter. Consider the closing of "The Marble Faun." We thought to catch sight of the blue sky at the close, but reckoned wrong. A haunting sense of uncertainty is on you at the close, as through the story. Donatello, Miriam, and Miriam's murdered shadow, what secret of theirs has been told you? Where the dead priest is we know. Graves can be found; but where the living Miriam and Donatello are, who can certify? We are like those who try to track travelers along a coast when their footprints have been washed out by the tide. We are baffled. All soul-life, I know, is mysterious, but this is not of that sort. This is the mystery of disease. Menace is in the air. We are neighboring with the abnormal.

And Hawthorne, as all dramatists, is a student of morals. You must have noticed how life never can grow great till it passes into the ethical. Bare intellect can never bind us prisoners to its car. But the ethical grasps us in hands of iron. We are as those who dream. Volition is ethics. Love is ethics. Conduct is ethics. Struggle is ethics. The quality of righteousness is on every field where battle waxes great. Moral issues engage us in Lear, in Valjean, in John Inglesant, and in Sidney Carton. If novelist or dramatist would throw us as a strong wrestler does, his appeal must be to the ethical. The moment life begins to grow, then is the scene shifted from the intellectual to the moral. What Hawthorne considers is, How do souls behave? "Spirit, what do you? Speak your motive." Right and conscience are themes pre-eminent, which hold mankind, and greet you here.

Nor must we neglect the literary setting of these psychological studies. And this naturally divides itself into two sections; namely, his style and his diversity. That Hawthorne's English is ideal has become an axiom. Dealing with the rudest passion, his style is never turgid. It flows on, flows deep, but is limpid always. Faultless language was one of his credentials. He was not Addisonian; Irving was that. He was himself. He created a style. Air is not more pellucid. I never read after him, that I do not see the stream far among the mountains, whose waters were never darkened save by the shadow of passing bird or cloud. Whatever he tells wins you, because of the beauty of his words. You have no doubt heard voices in the dark, which you wished might not hush because the music of them was so sweet. I feel so with Hawthorne. His work is as graceful as the tracery upon a winter's window.

Since the theme is essentially reduplicative in his various works, one would suppose Hawthorne would lack diversity. Nothing is remoter from the fact. He has instead given us captivating diversity. He never palls on us. I read not long ago all his works in immediate succession, so that the flavor of each lingered on the lip when all were ended; and my interest did not flag. This is the crucial test of variety. I did not seem looking at the same scenes, or on the same faces. And when we recall that in them all are the same forces operative so as to make each a reiteration of the other, the surprise increases. DuMaurier, whatever name he assigned the woman in his society cartoons, gave her the same face. All his women are twins. Sameness wearies us, like a drawling voice. But Hawthorne does not commit this sin. Every portrait stands out as individual as Hawthorne's own face. To instance a case: "Marble Faun," "House of the Seven Gables," and "The Scarlet Letter" are studies in conscience; yet they are so cunningly differentiated as to seem the literary progeny of different authors. That is art. We scarcely can conceive we are looking at the same face, but as the cast of Donatello at the hand of Kenyon, the face was the same, the resemblance easy to discover; still so different are they in characteristics, so changed is the expression in the two, as that, to the artist himself, it becomes barely believable the casts are meant for the same face. His faces are as the figure of the archangel Miriam would have repainted. He stood tall, strong, conquering, wonderful, unwounded, the dragon beneath his feet, but on his shield no dint that tells of battle fierce as death. Miriam would have painted the triumphant angel scarred, bleeding, with hacked shield and helmet, and with hacked and broken sword, and yet a conqueror still! Two faces and one personality.

Hawthorne's various works are to be studied by the dubious light of a diseased psychology. Souls in abnormal states are they all. "The Blythedale Romance" means hypnotism; "The House of the Seven Gables" means witchcraft; "Septimius Felton" means the elixir of life; "The Marble Faun" means a hybrid existence as animal-man; and "The Scarlet Letter" means conscience a consuming fire. We may agree on these being the central meanings of these great books. The characters few, the plot is brief and lacks intricacy. As stated, the fascination of Hawthorne does not consist in the story. The weird conception and the elaboration of character leave a silhouette lying like a deep shadow across the spirit. We can not well forget Hawthorne's characters. They seem graven with acids on the memory. They are weird, but not extravagant. Art lies in making the improbable seem probable. DeFoe has had no superior in this province. But the extravagant, as such, lacks, artistically. "Pilgrim's Progress" is an allegory truly, but so natural is it as to seem not parable but biography. Sometimes careless readers deem a treatment extravagant, which is rather most accurate portraiture. For instance, Stevenson's "The Strange Case of Dr. Jekyl and Mr. Hyde" has been classed as absurd and impossible by many readers who did not lack in intelligence; whereas, in a score of years, no book has been written more exactly true. Terribly, tragically true the story is. Not history nor biography has gotten so home to truth as this. Stevenson has written a theological volume and called it fiction, and it is the somber fact of too many souls. Evil indulged in masters the good with malignant certainty—this is the meaning of Jekyl and Hyde; and no one dares deny the fearful fact. So the seeming extravagant may be closest truth. This is true of Hawthorne's fictions. Unreal as they seem, they do touch us at every point. Let "The Blythedale Romance" stand for the malignant influence man may exercise on man; "The House of the Seven Gables" for the continued baneful effect of evil, and that a wicked man may cast a shadow black as midnight on a good life; "Septimius Felton" for the mind infatuated with a solitary idea become unbalanced and disqualified for service and manhood; and "The Scarlet Letter" for the doctrine that a good life is the only safe life. With such meanings, how rational and serviceable these weird tales become! He has told the common truths in such uncommon fashion as to write the moral across the sky of every soul. Hawthorne is a professor of moral philosophy, if you will. He is bringing the power of a superlative genius to enforce the truth that there is moral order in the world, and that sin is a violation of compact with your own soul. I shall always hold the superior novelist to be a potent teacher of the better. Our generation has had no more tragic lesson taught it than in "Anna Karenina." False to others, she became therein false to herself. Passion is not the first law of conduct. Duty sits higher at the feast than sex love. No writer on social ethics could have burned the validity of the marriage relation on the reason and conscience as this novel has done. Hawthorne is to be accounted a notable moral force. He thrusts home as Rustum did, when beside the Oxus he unwittingly fought with his son and slew him. So deep the spear had pierced Sohrab's side, to withdraw it was to die. And when we recall how easy it is to forget the weighty facts of observation and experience, the service rendered by those who make moral truths unforgetable, becomes worthy and memorable. Let us not be deceived; Hawthorne is as accurate as sunbeams. There are no new truths; but genius makes old truths seem new.

"Fanshawe" Hawthorne disowned, therefore for it no speech. "The Blythedale Romance" is a tale least like its author, and uses the machinery of the then current fiction. In the following regard, however, it was normal to the author's manner; it was a study of the abnormal, and the characters were that quaternion grown so familiar in the author's later works. The character of Hollingsworth is finely drawn. He is the vender of reforms. His pockets are full of them; and, like the pseudo reformer, the conditions of getting on with him are that you fall in with his fad. Zenobia's love is passion; and Priscilla is an apt picture of the results of a hypnotized subject. Hypnotism emasculates the will, and tends to reduce the free personality to the category of physical phenomena. Miles Coverdale, poet, is the one attractive actor on the stage, and the love of him, revealed at the last as the sun breaks through a cloud at setting, is in keeping with Hawthorne's daintiest execution.

But "The Scarlet Letter," "The Marble Faun," "The House of the Seven Gables," and "Septimius Felton," are masterpieces. They are cameos cut by some rare lapidary. One knows not which to admire the most. Each in its way seems to me perfect. There is no sunshine like that of Indian summer; and in these books we are walking in such a golden, mellow haze. "The Scarlet Letter" is a brave caption, as is "The House of the Seven Gables;" though we are told by James T. Fields that Fields had more to do with coining these titles than Hawthorne. But the result is justifying. We suspect romance from "The House of the Seven Gables." Tragedies look from the windows. "The Marble Faun" has about it a suspicion of delight; and "Septimius Felton" is a euphonious name for a fiction. "The Scarlet Letter" was the romance on which, as on a rock, the novelist's fame was builded. Its appeal met with instant response. Critics saw America had found a voice. A tragedy of conscience longer sustained than Macbeth is here, and one which ought to be compared with "Pippa Passes" and "Macbeth." Hester Prynne, with the scarlet letter blazing on her breast; little Pearl, elfin-like, dancing as sunbeams dance on troubled streams; Roger Chillingworth, dark, taciturn, injured, avenging, relentless, penetrating in his influence and insight, inexorable as fate, tenacious of his hate as death, masterful in his personality; and Arthur Dimmesdale, weak rather than wicked, sensitive, gifted with genius and the weakness which goes as the shadow of genius, a lover overborne of passion and a coward,—these are the *dramatis personæ* of a tragedy. Hester Prynne is woman the lover, faithful, injured, silent, wearing shame as if it were a crown, and not a cross; and, though loathed and branded by society, keeping love glowing in her heart like western windows smitten with the sun; watching her love from afar; not cursing nor despising him as he deserved, but, as women will, seeing his nobilities exalted and harboring no resentment. Dimmesdale afraid to take his place with Hester, but loving her; a saint in the world's thought, his eloquence growing fervid as tropic noon, he was an oracle. Eloquence sat upon his lips. Great passions broke across his spirit, as dashing waves. He was not bad, weak rather. Sinned, he had. He and Hester were joint criminals, she bearing her shame before the world; he canonized by that same world. Conscience cried aloud, "Bear shame with her;" and his spirit cried, "How can I? How can I?" But conscience spake on. Its speech never silenced. His life was living martyrdom. At last he seized the gibbet, where Hester Prynne had year by year stood a spectacle of shame, and called Hester and little Pearl to him, and showed his sin and penitence, and died. Fiction presents not many scenes likes Dimmesdale standing at night in the pillory of shame rehearsing his guilty and ghastly past. Nothing is forgotten. The Puritan sternness and purity, the attraction of love, which bound Hester to her dishonored home, the lack of sense of injury toward her husband Roger Chillingworth, the ship lying at anchor in which she and hers were to sail across the seas to liberty and love, the ship ready to sail, and

Dimmesdale, displaying his scarlet letter, sailing away on the ship of death,—this is tragedy!

Donatello is the central figure of "The Marble Faun," and might be set as an illustration of the evolutionary hypothesis. He is an importation of the beautiful Greek mythology. The faun was a Greek conception, part animal, part man. With the Greek all was animate. Plato taught the world had a soul. The Greek world was alive. Nymph, merman, naiad, every mountain and stream and sea had gods. The poesy of the notion was captivating; and the faun was a man having the hairy ears of a squirrel, and this was his bond to the animal world. The Greek received this current mythology with never a thought of its philosophy. All nature insensibly passed into life. The water's babbling was not inanimate, but rather the voices of the naiads. Beautiful the dream is; but the construction of a philosophy is quite another matter. This difficult task Hawthorne attempts in "The Marble Faun." And the subject for elaboration is, What shall awaken our laughing faun, Donatello, to manhood? Love does not do it. He is a part of nature, and moody like a pool over which glances the cloud, and in which laughs the sunshine. The carelessness of birds is on him. Forecast he does not know. Care and he are not brothers. But because of love for Miriam, Donatello becomes a murderer. Immediately his life is changed. He is murky as a sky filled with storms. Laughter is a forgotten art, joy a forgotten story; but he becomes a man. The faun is gone; the man is here. And the ethico-psychological question is raised, "Is sin necessary to manhood?" Did sin make Donatello a man? Was sin necessary to the evolution of character? Is sin an essential of progress? This is the question of "The Marble Faun." It clouds the sky, and fills the air with intimations of tempests. And this is a superior question of morals. And the reply is, Not sin made Donatello a man, but suffering. He needed awakening. A kiss awoke the sleeping beauty; but no kiss could rouse him. The sting of lash and cut of sword, —these must bring some spirits to themselves. And suffering roused Donatello to guess he was a man. With this interpretation, history is consonant. I have read somewhere the statement that "The Marble Faun" is nothing other than a guide-book to Rome. The criticism seems superficial in the extreme. As well say the ocean's office was to fling back sunlight. In this volume Hawthorne has given himself to a profound study, and as unique as profound. How shall a soul be stung to manhood? This is a dignified, not to say a sublime question. Conscience put Donatello on the rack. Suffering became a medicine to him. Crime is never essential to progress, though in the present system it would appear suffering is necessary. Who will deny manhood to be cheap at any price? Who will deny either that suffering has brought many a soul to its greater self? Eugenie Grandet, the one faultless character of Balzac, passed into a calm, sweet, wonderful womanliness through the ministry of suffering. Donatello might have suffered from unrequited love as Eugenie Grandet, and, like herself, have risen to high nobility of character. The chisel cuts shapeless marble into forms of imperishable loveliness; and suffering chisels spirit. Better manhood at any cost. Character is never costly when its worth is rightly conceived.

"Septimius Felton" is, to my mind, a stronger novel than usually allowed. In a sense, the work was left incomplete; but this was not in the story, rather in the minuter details. To all intents the novel is complete. Not a defect is apparent in the entire narrative. The English is exquisite. The style is chaste, even above the high average so natural to Hawthorne. Say with Riley,

"O, but the words were rainy sweet!"

Septimius Felton seems a younger Hamlet. He is scholar, and not afraid of action, yet shuns it. The inertia of thought stays his steps. The antithesis between scholar and soldier is finely brought out in the juxtaposition of Septimius Felton and Robert Hagburn; and, as always, Hawthorne does what he attempts, well. Felton is infatuated by the quest for the elixir of life. What a play for high powers is here afforded! A dim background of a dreamy past spent like a taper burnt out, in this self-same search, is mapped, as in "The House of the Seven Gables" the background of witchcraft is sketched. A consummate artist is Hawthorne, as any who ever attempted fiction. He has thrown a spell about you till you are as one walking in the land of lotus-eaters. The extent to which a mind may be absorbed in an idea is one of the surprises of psychology; and this tale paints a picture of a man thus absorbed. The bewitchment of the New World is added to the bewitchment of the Old in the admixture of Indian magic and herb wisdom as shown in Felton's aunt, and in the encounter between the young British officer and Felton, in which the officer succumbs to the prowess of the young American. In no one of his novels is the plot more cunningly laid than in this. Felton is immersed in his investigation. Like all dreamers, he is clutching the base of the rainbow's arch. To-morrow he will be immortal. How intoxicating visions are! Out of the grave where his slain foe lies buried, springs a flower which is to form the last ingredient of the elixir. One step more—and then? His heart leaps high like fountains. And meantime Sybil Dacy has come, come as a ghost, crept into his life; more, crept into his heart as shadows creep into an evening sky; and he finds himself a lover. The elixir is completed. They two shall drink. What is a solitary immortality? This wine of deathless life glows ruddy in the glass—and Sybil drinks, and when Septimius Felton reaches for the draught, she drops the glass upon the hearth, and shivers it to atoms. And all the precious liquor spilt! 'T is death, not life, crimsoned the goblet. Rankest poison, meant by her for him, was brewed. The elixir of immortality is here for drinking, and she has drunk some and spilled the rest. There is strange fascination in the story. I have not often been so thrilled as in reading it. Felton, intoxicated with his dream, now with his love, sees as lovers do but two, and a draught and immortality. And when he grasped at immortality he found he held in his hand death's garment instead. Sybil hating him, coming to avenge her lover's slaughter, loves him she came to slay, and drinks the deadly draught she meant for him. Love has one law. Not many passages in literature compare with the closing passages of Sybil Dacy's life. Hear her say with failing sight, "I thought I loved that youth in the grave yonder; but it was you I loved,— and I am dying. Forgive me for my evil purposes, for I am dying. Kiss me, thou poor Septimius, one kiss!" and as he stooped to do her bidding, she drew back. "No, there shall be no kiss! There may a little poison linger on my lips. Farewell!" Love and death's night!

"The House of the Seven Gables," written in less vivid colors than "The Scarlet Letter," is no less vivid a tragedy. The colors are grays. Twilight shadows all. At the last, and the last only, it lifts, and when lifted, lo, it is morning! The background of witchcraft gives the semblance of the unreal to all the tale. The antagonism of Pyncheon and Maule, dating from the poor man's being defrauded of his little all; the lordly Puritan dedicating his own house by his own tragic death; the baneful influence of a later Maule on sweet Alice Pyncheon; the perpetual memory of the prophecy of old Matthew Maule, "God shall give him blood to drink," until at last, like as the feud betwen Montague and Capulet might have been healed in a united Romeo and Juliet, this feud died in the marriage of Phœbe Pyncheon and Holgrave Maule,—surely this narrative is the creation of genius. But chief interest attaches to Clifford and Hepzibah Pyncheon and Judge Pyncheon. Reynolds painted no portraits so lifelike as these. There they sit. Judge Pyncheon complaisant, successful, ambitious, unscrupulous, selfish, tyrannical, suave, and rich. He is what Dimmesdale was not, a hypocrite.

He is bad, from heart to finger-tip. No light falls to relieve his character. He is murderer, and has thrown suspicion on his cousin Clifford, who was heir to the dead man's wealth, and is condemned to life imprisonment for a crime he did not commit; and Clifford Pyncheon falls heir to a blasted name, a ruined life, and finally to a dazed intellect. He is a ship, wrecked on the reef, Judge Pyncheon. The condemned man was sensitive, and in his temperament eminently artistic. He was sensuous. Physical beauty or ugliness smote on him, as a hand on an instrument. Pure, he had yet lacked character, which is, in itself, a fortress not to be taken by assault, and in prison broke under his load of shame, and became a harmless madman. But Hepzibah his sister, had believed in him, and loved him through all. She never wavered, seeing with woman's insight that not Clifford, but the Judge, was the real murderer. At last the poor shadow of what once was a man crept back unawares to the House of the Seven Gables. There, in poverty, loneliness, pride, and sore disgrace, Hepzibah Pyncheon has lived these years alone. Life meant to her, Clifford. In the vocabulary of her heart was but one word. Her days are wasted like spent sunshine. Clifford at home once more, mad, helpless as a child, is disturbed in his sense of sensuous beauty by his sister's homely face and her shambling movement, at which her dear eyes dim with tears. In her heart is sacrifice sweet as heaven. God, looking at her, grows glad. An echo to her brother's need, Hepzibah Pyncheon is a woman so homely, brave, beautiful in soul, as to make one in love with all womanhood for her dear sake.

The death of Judge Pyncheon in the hour of his highest honor is a touch of genius, not less wonderful than Arthur Dimmesdale's death, though totally unlike it. This is a study in conscience, as "The Scarlet Letter." In Dimmesdale, conscience had burned the scarlet on his bosom. But Judge Pyncheon is conscienceless, as if he had been not man, but brute. He was his own divinity. Not a sole virtue touches him to beauty. Not a flower blooms on this sterile rock. There is something worse than suffering from conscience, and that is not to suffer at all, to have moral paralysis, to be let alone of God, and so take one's own way down to hell. Better a thousand-fold be Arthur Dimmesdale than Judge Pyncheon. Dimmesdale stands on a scaffold, and his world sees him; so he dies. But Pyncheon, with his hidden sin, dies alone. He sits, quiet, nothing disturbs him—he is dead. The house is empty, the night comes on, the tick of his watch in his hand is the solitary whisper in the silence; still he stirs not. Day dawns, the sunlight creeps across his face, the watch runs down—and silence, silence! God hath left him; he is dead.

These be the creations of one dreamer's brain; and having seen and heard them, their tragedy completed, we turn away, knowing Nathaniel Hawthorne was a genius of such commanding sort as Literature has seldom named among her votaries.

Shakespeare's Women

SHAKESPEARE'S women are the world's women. Provincialism and cosmopolitanism exist in literature as in life. The provincial writer delineates a local type. He is as the old masters, who, though painting the Madonna, produced a Dutch, German, or Italian face, according as the artist belonged to the Flemish, German, or Italian school. He painted the women he knew. Our provincial writer gives the characters he knows. The cosmopolitan writer does no more. He gives us those he knows; but his friendships are as the horizons of the world. They embrace the planet. Shakespeare must, through all ages, remain the type of universal genius. The lute he holds is not of English make. I conceive Charles Dickens to be the master of English types; to this day he is unapproachable. He knows the fiber of English character best and worst; and an acid criticism of Charles Dickens's delineations will be in essence a like criticism of English character. Squeers, Uriah Heep, Smike, Copperfield, and Sidney

Carton are indigenous to English soil. And Shakespeare knows England, but is not English. Walter Savage Landor has acutely observed,

"Shakespeare is not our poet, but the world's."

He knows Englishmen. His characterizations are as exact as photography. Falstaff, the duke of Bedford, Edmund the Bastard, Richard II, Edward I, Henry VIII, are like as life; his coloring, his figures, his background, his self-revelation of character, are worthy the artist; but when he has given us the canvas filled with English figures, wassail, war, comedy, tragedy, ringing laughter, and blind Lear's cry of anguish, the artist has scarce begun his creative work. Dickens is at home in England; in America and Venice he is a traveler; but Shakespeare was by birth a citizen of the world, and by chance a citizen of England. In Troy, in Greece, in Rome, in mediæval Italy, in Denmark, in Scotland—in each his dialect seems that of a native. He knows not Englishmen alone, but men. Othello, Timon, Caliban, Prospero, Mark Antony, Falstaff, Macbeth, Lear, Shylock, Iago, Antonio, Hamlet,—these all seem as men eager to whisper their dearest secret in this poet's ears.

From these observations, accurate in point of truth, it will follow that Shakespeare's women are the world's women, thus recurring to the proposition with which this article set out. And how large a business is in hand becomes apparent. This is larger traffic than Prince Hur's argosies ever brought to Simonides' wharves at Antioch on the sea. In literature and life woman is a central figure. Men and women are joint actors on every stage where comedy laughs like love on wedding morning, or tragedy bleeds like Hamlet on a crimsoned sand. Women and men are protagonists. They are as similar as stars, they are as dissimilar as middle night and middle day. The psychology of man is the psychology of woman; the psychology of woman is so unlike that of man as that for the two, different disquisitions must be written. Woman is woman in the finest fiber of body and spirit. Man and woman stand at opposite quarters of the sky; and are as Cassiopeia and Orion looking forever into each other's eyes. The qualities of sex are wrought into the very texture of the soul, and are as ineradicable as the properties of matter. Of man and woman we say they are counterparts. These two give all the material of tragedy or joy. They are as necessary each to the other as voice to echo, and echo to voice. As far apart as the diameter of the skies, they are still so near as that their leaning lips may touch. Love is life's sweet commonplace, because Ferdinand and Miranda possess mutual attraction like the tug that pulls the stars together. It is an old history, this record of woman's power. So long as men are men, so long will women be

"A thing of beauty and a joy,"

but likewise a creature of unexploited powers. Love knows strange witchery and mastery. Merlin and Vivien are portraits hanging on the walls of every age. The world's first morning had its Epithalamium, even as has its golden afternoon.

But in fealty to history be it said that woman's part in the world's doings is a growing part. The Orient and the early Occidental world saw her with veiled face. But now, as is legitimate, the veil is fallen from her eyes. It is not meet that beauty such as hers should hide its face. It is not possible to estimate the value of beauty. Beautiful womanhood is God's visible æsthetics, fairer than a Titian or a Rembrandt. The beautiful tales of early love —of Jacob and Rachel, of Boaz and Ruth— are lovely as an evening sky, yet in them is a sensible lack. Woman seems not to be a legitimate figure in the scene. She seems not wholly planned for in the artist's thought. The picture, in other words, seems not to have been painted with her in mind, as a momentous figure on his canvas. It is only in later days she stands in her own right, upon the foreground of the scene. The Angelus has interpreted the better times aright. The solemn evening, the distant spire from which the music of the evening thrills, the toil not yet completed, and in the foreground, for whose sake the background is, a man and a woman— a woman and a man, with bowed heads under the falling night. Man, woman, and God are the participants in this solemn scene.

The ancient tragedy must always lack, because woman has not a legitimate place. Her unjust subordination strikes us with a sense of misproportion we can not get rid of. In Homer's epic, while for Helen, Trojan and Greek, between Samos and Scamander, crossed spears in swirl of battle, Helen has scarce a presence or a voice; and the parting of Hector and Andromache marks the disparity of man and woman, so that you leave the pathetic picture with a sense of dissatisfaction. Not Rome nor Athens knew woman as man's antithesis and equal. The restoration of woman to herself and man was to belong to the miracle Jesus wrought for all the world.

Singular how long it took men to learn the painting of a woman's face! The Greek ideal woman was Juno, or Venus, or Phryne. Homer tells us of the "ox-eyed Juno." The perfect bust, figure, face, the outline faultless, the eyes as dreamy as an Indian summer afternoon,—these were the symptoms of a woman's beauty as the Greek artist hewed her from the marble or made her glow on canvas. The Venus of Milo is illustrative—a faultless form, a face carved by beauty's perfect rule, and yet a soulless face. That was Greek misconception of womanhood. She had no soul; hers was a sensuous beauty. Ænone, deserted on Ida's mountain, weeping for her Paris, not less nor more, is all Greek poesy can give. It was the Madonna taught the artist a new and right ideal of woman's face, and so the world a new idea of woman. The dreamer painted her again, again, again. Each effort was an imperceptible advance. No Venus form will prove adequate for Mary's immortal beauty. Venus had a lover, Mary had a babe; and there was the necessary intuition that this woman, this Mary, would not simply be a perfect form, with Oriental richness flooding brow and cheek, for she was groping after the invisible, she was feeling after God; and at the last the mediæval masters found the secret, and painted woman with a soul. And from that day the world's idea of a woman's beauty has been revolutionized. No dryad on the mountain, nor nereid in the laughing sea, nor a Diana at the chase with quiver and with bow, in queenly grace like marble glowing with the tints of life, but woman, beautiful, spirituelle, yet human.

And with this idea the largest art must deal. There is a sense of lack in Antigone; there is no sense of lack in Robert Browning's Colombe. In the old-time figure there is immaturity; in the recent face and form there is maturity and unconscious queenliness. And with the interpretation of woman as thus conceived, every poet, whether in prose or verse, has to do. It seems his necessary calling. Dante and Petrarch have heard the voice whose music was sweeter than siren's song, and Beatrice and Laura are earnests of a right and therefore high conception of regenerate womanhood. And we must know how crowded is the Pantheon of modern literature with woman's figures. Each genius must attempt this subtle analysis. Dickens has in the main made his women weak. With the exception of Little Dorrit and Agnes, you will scarcely call to mind a magnetic woman in all that company of female portraitures—children of a fertile imagination. Thackeray's good women are weak, or at most not strong; his strong women are wicked. Becky Sharp has few equals as a delineation—more the pity, she is so bad. How to be deplored that Colonel Newcome and Henry Esmond have not women of kindred nobility and strength. In Mary Collett and Constance, Shorthouse has given us with lavish generosity. George Eliot has in Maggie Tulliver and Romola served her kind only less essentially than in Adam Bede and Daniel Deronda. Hawthorne's Hester Prynne must remain one of the triumphs of romancist's power, and stand a protest of living strength and nobility to poor, nervous Arthur Dimmesdale. Tolstoi's Anna Karenina has not been excelled in audacious attempt at portrayal of woman's passion in a hundred years. As a rule, Hall Caine's women have not the strength his men possess. Tennyson has been lavish in his contribution to the literature of womanhood. Ænone, Mariana, Enid, Guinevere, Annie, Elaine, the Princess, Godiva, Eleanore,—this is no simple list of names, but rather a collection of portraits which Sir Joshua Reynolds had not known the skill to paint. Longfellow gave us Evangeline; and Browning, with characteristic prodigality of genius, which minds us of the wealth of gifts the summer gives, has dowered womanhood. He is a realist, and has given us good and bad, but has not obscured goodness with evil. Evelyn Hope, Mildred, Pippa, Pompilia, Colombe, Fatima,—these are among the voices for whose words the poet makes a silence. Edmund Spenser hath left us Una, the poet's dream of purity in an age impure.

But what of Shakespeare's women? Has the essayist forgotten them? Is this prelude? No, rather this is an integral section of the discussion, and not irrelevant matter.

All pictures have background. All discussion has relations. Shakespeare's work must stand in contact with the work of others. A poet once having given his dreaming to the world has no power to slay his progeny. The creations of his fancy will live for centuries after the poet's burial; and the product of any genius must stand beside the product of all genius. There is no isolation here. All vital literature, like shipwrecked king, prince, duke, courtiers, and sailors in "The Tempest," tend toward a single point, and there hold convocation. Time has no place in such regal gathering. The earliest writings are read by the light of the latest dawn; and Shakespeare's creations must stand alongside the achievement of all centuries which preceded him. He is in the mesh, inextricably woven. And besides this, there is in him an anachronism necessary and apparent. The flavor of an age will cling to all a poet's creation. He sees the world, but through the air which surrounds him. In consequence, a modern poet's portrait of a Grecian woman is not altogether accurate. She is colored with hues the ancients knew not how to mix. This is in particular true of notions of women. Shakespeare's women are resultants of sixteen Christian centuries. They are not statues, they are not bovine-eyed, they are not attendants, but equals, of man. Shakespeare is not aware that the unconscious attitude of his women is redolent of the Christ elevation of the sex. His Cressida, in her flavor of womanhood, belongs not to the age of Priam, king of Troy, but to the age of Elizabeth, queen of England.

It is Shakespeare's triumph that his actors live, and act because they live. They are not puppets, nor yet are they powdered semblances. We had rather doubt the personality and power of Napoleon than the personality and power of Hamlet. That shadow at Elsinore, through which a dagger might be plunged, and not a drop of blood be let, is more substantial than Napoleon with the Lombard's iron crown encircling his brow. Shakespeare's women are alive. Their voices are articulate joy or despair. Titania coddling the poor mechanic, Bottom, so blind she is with love, holds not a hint of fiction, but seems fact hard as the core of granite hills. Ariel seems scarce a myth. But if the fairies seem substantial, what crimson blood will tinge the cheek, make ruddy the lip, and thrill the frame of mortals with bounding and tumultuous life! Assembled here upon this tessellated pavement and under the gorgeous roof of Shakespeare's creation, see our pageant: Hermia, Miranda, Helena, Julia, Sylvia, Francisca, Mistress Ford, Margaret, Dame Quickly, Adriana, Hero, Mariana, Beatrice, Rosaline, Jessica, Katharine, Rosalind, Olivia, Katharine the Shrew, Viola, Hermione, Perdita, Constance, Lady Percy, Volumnia, Virginia, Juliet, Lady Macbeth, Cleopatra, Octavia, Portia, Gertrude, Ophelia, Emilia, Desdemona, Imogen, and—but why prolong the list? The room seems crowded even now, and through the open door I see them coming still, an apparently interminable procession. How strange a company this is! We shall not see its like again. Trojan, Greek, Roman, Venetian, Illyrian, Sicilian, French, Goth, and Jew—but women all, with but one speech, and that of woman. But how strange a company! The queen is here, the princess, the lady, the maid, the life as spotless as the lily, the hand all stained with blood; the wench, garrulous and foul; the shrew, the heart of lust, shameless ingratitude, beautiful filial devotion, wifely fidelity, maternal love, shrewdness, unquestioning trust, ambition towering like a mountain, grief that will not be assuaged, love that thinks it but a trivial thing to die, heroisms framed to make life magnificent, littleness which brings blush to cheek and forehead, the bold wanton, the modesty as sweet as the blooming of violets in the woods, virginhood, wifehood, maternity, penury, plenty, affluence, regnant queen, banishment and solitude, each day a living fear, each night a nightmare, or rest and quiet like a sky at night,—all are here; and the amazement of it all is, one artist is the creator of all this motley, marvelous company. These are types, but types of the race. Shakespeare has taken us so that, as within a temple, we may look against the light, and see the arabesques of beauty. This is genius in the delineation of character, most of all of woman's character. We can not comprehend a woman's doings by seeing the acts. We must be imported, must become central in the life of which the acts are peripheral. Thus, and thus only, do we catch the movement of the spirit. Here we note the fascination of art in Shakespeare's exhibit of feminine character. We seem not to be spectators. The spectator looks on; in Shakespeare we take part. The doings of the actors seem as native to them as shadows to the hills. Its *rationale* is apparent. That Lady Macbeth had done as she is represented is axiomatic, so completely has Shakespeare's genius taken us captive. We become so *en rapport* with the actor as that a different course of conduct seems unimaginable. Then these women are women; they are natural, not mechanical. They are individual; their identity is like that of morning and the sky. Shakespeare does not duplicate. Study an artist's canvas, and you will likely find the signs of a Corot, Millais, or Inness. They are much as the painter described in Armorelle of Lyonesse, who had many canvases but a single face, with the sea always as background to her single figure. But Shakespeare has no favorites. He can no more repeat himself than nature can. His creations are as distinct, personal, and consonant as if they had grown. He seems as an improvisatrice, who can not reproduce a given extemporization, seeing it has gone from her. Here is boundless fertility of creation. Lovers and lovers there are among his lovely women, but they are not echoes. Each is as certainly a voice with pitch, cadence, individual charm, as any voice you can recall among the dearest your ears have heard.

We must study in masses. The necessary brevity of this article precludes extended portraiture. Individual characterization is not possible, but we may take classes and study them as a painter his cloud effects. So call up some lovers among these women gathered under Shakespeare's roof. Goneril, Miranda, Ophelia, Jessica, Juliet, Cleopatra, Octavia, Desdemona, Imogen. Each is distinct and individual. They are not simply different names, but different people. You find no difficulty in distinguishing them, as with the two Dromios, in "The Comedy of Errors." Each stands out distinct, like a mountain against the sky; and of each we feel that she is adequate; and when you see a woman loving, you will find her prototype among Shakespeare's womenkind. Allow a hasty and imperfect characterization of those whose names are written here. Goneril, unchaste, traitor to husband and father, enamored of a braggart and villain, who is no more true to her than she is to others; Goneril, flushed with the fever of passion, knowing how to love with a heart of fire,—she is as Swanhild in Eric

Bright-eyes, whose character you deplore, but for whose love you feel compassion. Miranda is pure as the white cloud, drifting high in the blue summer skies. Leal she is, as day to dawn. Being love, pure, sweet, unquestioned, she is fidelity embodied. Ophelia loved, striving against love, filled with doubt of Hamlet where doubt had no occasion, and, maddening, went love-lorn to her death. Jessica is love-engrossed, hearing naught besides Lorenzo's poet eloquence:

> "How sweet the moonlight sleeps upon this bank!
> Here will we sit, and let the sounds of music
> Creep in our ears; soft stillness and the night
> Become the touches of sweet harmony.
> Sit, Jessica."

Juliet esteems Romeo greater wealth than worlds. Cleopatra is passion in peerless beauty. Octavia is fidelity of love, that suffers and loves on. Desdemona is love faithful as stars, misjudged, but only loyal still; and her pleadings with Othello for but another day of life are among the voices of tragedy which never hush. Imogen is love that believes, and loves, and keeps the heart with but a single door. If Leonatus come not, then is life bereft indeed. Estimates these, but estimates that fall short of conveying the idea of character. The subtle but incommunicable beauty we can no more rehearse than describe the dawning of the day.

Woman is capable of extremes of nobility or evil. Regan, Tamora, Lady Macbeth, disclose Shakespeare's knowledge of the depravity possible to woman's nature. Regan is ingratitude. Tamora is the Iago of Shakespeare's women. Lady Macbeth is the woman of the world, who will bear no obstacle between her and the coveted goal. This power of a woman for evil has no more potent representative in fiction than this queen, with the ineradicable bloodstains on her hands. Queen Gertrude was weak rather than vicious; and is a nonpareil study in vacillating womanhood. Constance stands for mother-love, sleepless, untiring; Cordelia for daughterly self-sacrifice and devotion, so beautiful that, long as crazed Lear tears his white locks in the dark night of storm, there will Cordelia stand the symbol of fidelity, as true as heaven.

One phase of woman's strength Shakespeare did not portray; one, too, which had given room for all that prodigality of power this arch-genius of our world possessed. I refer to the religious spirit. Woman is essentially devout. She feels the secret of the Divine. She is a worshiper, and women are always chief among the devotees at any altar. Devotion to God is the noblest passion of the soul. It leads to unapproachable heights of heroism and purity; and had this master painted womanhood beneath the shadow of Christ's cross, he had completed the circle of human life.

Shakespeare has given us the world. The heart of man and woman alike he reads as if an open book before his eyes. And it is inspiring to recall that he has left us a gallery of noble women,

> "Whose loveliness increases
> And can never pass to nothingness."

He has given us the bawd, the wanton, the frozen heart, the cruel and inexorable will, the weak, vacillating virtue,—all these plague-spots he has seen and pictured. He saw all, painted all. He was faithful as the sun in taking pictures. And in a former day I have wished Shakespeare had not given us Falstaff and Mistress Quickly, but now I am glad for all. The exhaustless fertility of resource is evidenced in this, as in no other way. Shakespeare saw the abysms of shame as well as the tall hills of grace and purity, and portrayed all. Woman is wicked as well as virtuous; and he who would glass her for others' eyes must not evade this unsavory portraiture. It is a false psychology as well as ethics, which denies the evil. We can not abolish sin by bald declaration. But this Shakespeare does; he leaves the impression that woman wicked is woman abnormal. He gives holy intimation that woman normal is woman noble, and so leaves us enamored with womanhood. This is a major service for manhood, because historically a high estimate of woman is a necessary antecedent to an exalted manliness in either individual or race.

In one of his sonnets, Shakespeare says:

"Full many a glorious morning have I seen
    Flatter the mountain-top with sovereign eye,
Kissing with golden face the meadows green,
    Gilding pale streams with heavenly alchemy."

And when a study of Shakespeare's women is concluded, it leaves a sense as of such immortal morning on our spirits. We have uplift, vision, help.

The Deserted Village

THIS is Oliver Goldsmith's chief literary merit—he helped to bring poetry back to itself. Epochs of poetry are like dynasties of kings. Their genius dissipates. Strength gives place to weakness. With Pope and Dryden poetry had become artificial. Those poets were masters of rhyme and movement. Pope's verse was as the billow's rock, save that each couplet gave the identical beat of its predecessor. Variety ceased to have a place. Nor was this the only or chief fault. These writers had immured poetry in palaces. Parnassus had ceased to be a mountain, and had come to be a lady's boudoir or a king's antechamber. Clearly this would dry up the saps of inspiration. Poetry belongs under the open sky, beside the momentous sea, and in the solemn silences of night-time and the stars, or with the tragedy and destiny of souls. These things are worthy. The tawdry tinsel of court-life affords no sufficient theme for poetry. It may suffice for the poetaster, but will not satisfy the poet. Goldsmith, living in the literary era following the supremacy of Pope, found himself in the ebb-tide of that method. The tide was moving, but not passed out. It lapped the sands, and trembled for departure. In the age lorded over by that rugged genius, Dr. Johnson, the influence of Addison, Pope, and Dryden was still potent, and all but omnipotent.

Ragged and rugged as was the strength of Boswell's hero, he hewed no path for his own feet. His prose is manufactured. It has no distinct personality. It passes credence that such a man as we know Johnson to have been would tolerate the bondage of mere nicety. Yet in that style he wrote, though his spirit must have been a constant rebel against its narrowness; and "Lives of the Poets" and "Rasselas" are written in such balanced sentences as present us a dignified contribution to the Addisonian style. In the "Lives of the Poets," not Milton is the hero, but a Dryden or a Pope. This seems incredible, yet is simply true. Not might, but method, was the gauge of merit in that dead day.

And into such a literary inheritance Goldsmith came. He was gambler, dandy, bacchanal; he was idle, desultory in study and in movements; he was strolling minstrel, earning a doubtful crust from peasants with his flute; he was consecutively student of law, theology, medicine; he was tutor in a gentleman's family, then usher in a school, then druggist's clerk, then strolling player, then beggar, and a failure in all save dissipation. Who could well conceive a more unsavory life? A vagabond was Goldsmith; and a vagabond in propensions he remained until he died. But after a fashion he came to himself at last. He found his powers. His weaknesses clung to him as affectionately as his homeliness, and at length brought him to his grave. But Goldsmith was no martyr, rather the victim of his own follies. An egregious blunderer his whole life through, he was lucid only in writing. His "Vicar of Wakefield" is a classic among novels; and what was meant to save him from a debtor's prison, has wrought the larger service of keeping him from the prison-house of oblivion.

His fame as poet rests on two poems. Besides these, he wrote scarcely another worthy bit of verse; but to be author of "The Traveler" and "The Deserted Village" is not to be a plebeian, even in the royal realm of poetry.

Who speaks of "The Deserted Village" intelligently, must approach it in this method. The "Who?" and "What?" always bear with heavy weight on any production. If we are to understand a literary theme, we must come to it with knowledge. With many of Robert Browning's noblest poems we are completely in the dark, if we be not furnished with an explanatory clause. When this is supplied, the poem comes to be a revelation. This word of explanation, while not so necessary in the case of "The Deserted Village," is still a requisite for its best understanding. In it Goldsmith's service to English poetry becomes apparent. It is a long way from the "Rape of the Lock" to "The Deserted Village;" and in this contribution we have the first declaration for the natural as contradistinguished from the artificial. In other words, in this poem we are coming out under the open sky once more; and poetry has ceased to be apathetic, and has found again the cunning of fingering the stops of the lute of life. The poem is open to criticism on the ground of congruity. It is incongruous. The village described is English; but the eviction described is Irish. Nor is the nightingale a bird that sings in Ireland at all.

though represented as making its plaint over desolated Auburn. Besides this, the political philosophy is erroneous, as has often been pointed out. Commerce, with its postulate of wealth, is not a hurt, but a help. These criticisms are just, and a critique of the poem may not pass them by in silence.

Allowing the criticisms to be admissible, there is a larger truth; and it is this: The poem, as a whole, is a delight. Its immediate success was phenomenal. "The Traveler" had prepared the way for "The Deserted Village;" and Irving, in his "Life of Goldsmith," observes, "Its sale was instantaneous and immense." Repeated editions were called for within a few days. There was a hungry public; and the heart-element in the tale was satisfying. "The Traveler" is the more perfect poem; "The Deserted Village" the more popular one. The former was philosophic; the latter was domestic; and the same causes which have conduced to the popularity of Ian Maclaren, Barrie, and Thomas Nelson Page wrought in behalf of "The Deserted Village."

In versification, the style was that of Pope. The *motif* was as foreign to Pope as meadows fresh with flowers and grass and mosses, to the desert blistered in the sun. In other words, in form Goldsmith was still under the dominancy of the late literary autocrat; but in spirit he had shown himself a leader, and had been a helper in bringing English poetry back unto its own. "The Deserted Village" is pastoral poetry; and preludes a century of poetry in which no element of strength, grace, naturalness, or beauty was wanting.

The home sentiment is the affluent thought of the poem. To that, attribute the tenacious hold these words have had on the heart and memory of the English-speaking world. The Saxon is leal to hearth and native land. The potent element in "Evangeline" is the grip on our sympathies gained by the expatriation of the Acadians. We revolt against the tyranny and inhumanity. The same fact with a different setting is presented in "The Deserted Village." Thus runs the tale: Where once stood

"Sweet Auburn, loveliest village of the plain,"

in quietude, plenty, beauty, joy; where once rang the laughter of merrymaking, and stood the home, the genial inn, the village preacher's modest mansion, the school-house with memories of ferule and fun, now desolation saddens all the scene.

> "No more the grassy brook reflects the day,
> But choked with sedges works its weedy way;"

and the cause is the eviction of tenants by a proprietor, that he might inclose the farms in his own private domain. Such the story of "The Deserted Village;" and pathetic it is. It touches the sentiments; and Goldsmith makes this the opportunity for inveighing against luxury that grows with wealth, and wealth that grows with commerce.

Better to lay the purposed moral aside, and forget the intent of the poet. The world has found its chief concern in the unaffected grace and pathos with which home-life and heart-life have been depicted. The case becomes our own. We turn with fondness at the heart, and tears in the eyes toward the home of childhood. The tenacity of affection with which renters in the Old World cling to the farm on which generations of a single name have grown, until they seem rooted to the soil like the hawthorn, can not be appreciated in our newer continent, where domestic life dawned but yesterday.

Yet are childhood's remembrances the same with all of us. Each heart turns gladly back to the old home; and he has looked on age with unpardonable indifference who has not noted now, as men grow older, the heart clings more lovingly to the old home, to the old memories, to the old paths. This is the major fascination of "The Deserted Village." The verse runs quiet, like some silent river drowsing toward a not distant sea. We drift upon it. The story touches our better memories and our better natures; and it seems safe to become prophetic in declaring that no day will dawn when those who read English literature will pass "The Deserted Village" without tenderness and tears.

George Eliot as Novelist

ANGLO-SAXON literature has made surprising revelations of power. Coming late, when all the lists seemed filled, it yet made for itself room. It was as the black knight in "Ivanhoe," unexpected; and once entered the lists, its powers, as his, were unexploited, and the disclosure of them came as the discovery of a new constellation. No form of literature but has been attempted by this race. Each seemed a challenge. Romance poetry,—who like Edmund Spenser? The epic,—has not blind Milton become a chief musician like blind Homer? Lyric poetry,—have we not that rare lyrist, Alfred Tennyson? And in drama, Shakespeare answers the challenge of Æschylus, and takes the laurel from that gray head, and puts it on his own ruddy locks. Prose has received no nobler contributions than those of Hooker, Milton, Burke.

The audacity of genius has characterized these literary attempts. Nothing has daunted this new knight. Not Launcelot was so inconquerable in the lists. The Greek, with his affluence of genius, had wrought in every department of letters save the novel. He wrote fiction in drama, or epic, or narrative poem. These were "Tales of the Wayside Inn," or oftener of court and camp; yet with the enlargement of the story-teller's hearing through printing, poetry became too narrow a path; and Marlowe and Spenser gave their pens to Blackmore and Thackeray. I am of opinion that not since men listened to tale in Arab's tent by fountain-side under the stars, has imagination been so universally eager for a voice as now. There have been eras when the fancy was wilder, when the world seemed unhindered to the shore of the remotest sea, when the imagination ran more readily and easily to the extravagant; but never a time when chaste and vivid imagination could boast such constituency as now. Men would have the prose of life lapse into poetry, as the quiet brook into music of waterfall. They refuse to be held at the mill of toil, and are as impatient of fetters as a king's son in chains. The lordlier life within must have speech. Spirit will dream, and ask another how to dream. Love whispers in every ear. Men, women, youth, age— love kisses the sleeping lips of each, and thrills them to an awakening. Man was never more conscious of heart-hunger than now; and fiction is an answer to this cry for bread.

The novel is the certain sign that we are not lapsed into commercial serfdom. The demand for fiction is a good sign. Let us not imagine otherwise. Prurient stories, in themselves ill omens, are still an evidence of this passion for imagination. They constitute a misapplication of a divine power. The what we see and are will not suffice. To this truth bear all novels witness. Ulysses was

"Always roaming with a hungry heart;"

but Ulysses was brother to us all. Discoveries, voyagings, pageants, searchings for the holy grail, heroisms greater than Hector's,— all wander in the heart like winds across a moor. We stand ready, a watcher at an eastern window, waiting for the dawn. We will not sleep, supposing night will never cease. And fiction touches us here. It bids us know audacities of love, fidelity, heroism, suffering, are never dead, and are not of yesterday. They live to-day. They neighbor with us, and we know it not. The face of age masks an immortal love. That scarred cheek could tell a tale of noble daring fitted to the heart, as if it were harpstrings smitten by a harper's hand. This, I take it, is the essential meaning of the novel; and if so, who could deny the native nobility of this mode of expression?

And it has been the good fortune of the Saxon to produce the two most representative women of literature, Elizabeth Barrett Browning and George Eliot; the one the greatest woman poet, the other the greatest woman novelist. While true, George Eliot wrote a volume of poems, as also one of essays, she is to be classed neither as poet nor essayist, but as novelist. She came into an era rendered illustrious by Dickens and Thackeray. She must hang her light in a sky lit with two suns. The attempt was one of splendid daring. No single age had produced two such writers of fiction. Indeed, few names are to be mentioned in the same catalogue. Scott, Balzac, Hawthorne, Hugo, Tolstoi, Thackeray, Dickens,—what hinders this catalogue to be practically complete? And into lists where these knights rode came George Eliot. Thackeray saw and heralded her genius. Genius will make a place, not find one. Genius does not ask a constituency, but creates one; and that is better.

I think it safe to affirm woman's powers are better adapted to the novel than any other form of literature. Lecky was doubtless right in this observation. Woman's gift of fine feeling and noble passion can speak with native strength here as nowhere else. George Eliot is a distinguished example of what a woman can do in this field; and yet let it be remembered that her work is as strictly masculine as her pseudonym. Her writings do not bear the marks of femininity. Had she kept her incognito, her sex would scarcely have been guessed. However, in her undervaluation of women there is something feminine. Hetty is bad; Gwendolyn Harleth is weak; the betrothed of Silas Marner is fickle; the heroine of Middlemarch is not strong, to say the least; Romola, the chiefest of her women, is lacking in some qualities certainly indigenous to womanhood. But woman is given a better part than in any other female novelist.

Eliot does not write stories, but rather psychological or social studies. She has written no romance fascinating as "Jane Eyre." Charlotte Brontë knew the art of telling a tale

as George Eliot did not. In my conviction,
Elizabeth Stuart Phelps is her superior in the
same regard. But neither does Thackeray's
strength lie in story-telling. His story lags
like a sleepy urchin, though in "Henry Esmond" he has shown us what powers were at
his command, for it bears us on as a wave;
and "Quentin Durward" is not more magic in
its movement. Consider our authoress's merits. "Midlemarch" drowses. "Silas Marner"
is a gem of pastoral in prose, idyllic, simple,
inartificial, sweet as new-mown meadows at
night, redemptive in tone and effect. "Adam
Bede" is a repugnant study in conscience and
religion, never rising to the fascinating, but
always running at high levels in its humor,
insight, discrimination, and probing of the
soul. "Felix Holt" is a study in labor, and is,
much as the purely purpose fiction is likely to
be, heavy. "Daniel Deronda" is, all in all, the
most attractive and enchaining story this authoress has told. The movement has a swing
like a wave, the love is contagious; the character of Gwendolyn Harleth is disappoint-
ing, but accurate; Myra artless, attractive, and
compelling interest; Lapidoth, an exact portrait of a shameless, debased soul; Mordecai

is magnetic in his fervor, and thrilling in his finer sense of soul. "Romola" is a mediæval romance, catching admirably both tone and temper of the Savonarola era, and giving a clear insight into the Florence of Lorenzo the Magnificent. The story told leaves you in shadow like a sky suddenly overcast, but you are sure you have read a great book.

Comparison between George Eliot and Mrs. Humphrey Ward will serve to bring out the qualities of the former; and it seems clear that the niece of Matthew Arnold has as certainly taken Eliot for her pattern as Dante did Virgil. The peculiarity of imitation is that the imitator catches the weakness, but not the strength of the original. Such is the case in this instance. Mrs. Ward apparently aims at giving a study, rather than writing a story. She affects philosophy, political economy, theology. She possesses none of the story-teller's art. Her novels are voluminous, tedious, lack movement, and do not rivet attention. You never become interested so as to be loath to lay the volume down. "Robert Elsmere," "Marcella," "Sir George Tressady," are not commonly interesting, but uncommonly long and tiresome. They lack in dramatic power, and have no notion of climax. There is scant movement, little color, and an unpleasant sense of the physician who will insist on inoculating you irrespective of your need. She proposes a study; but those who propose this sort of fiction must be gifted with genius, and that of a high order. Thackeray may sermonize if he will, because his rambling utterances are a delight. Balzac may give studies, because he is a marvelous photographer of society conditions. Dickens may give a study in poverty, and name it "Oliver Twist," because he knows the art to subordinate the purpose to the movement of the narrative, and illumines all the path with the light of that varied genius which used him as amanuensis. So may George Eliot give a study of domesticity in "Middlemarch," or of hard human nature in "Mill on the Floss," because she is a great novelist, because she has penetrative vision, constructive ability, and consummate grasp of character. Contrast her work with Mrs. Ward's, and the difference is an unbridgeable chasm.

The tragic element in "Adam Bede" is growing in interest to the close, and in "Mill on the Floss" the scene of that flood in whose mad waters Tom and Maggie Tulliver find a grave, but find love, too, when seeing the beautiful forgiveness on which he has no claim, Tom cries "Magsie!" and then, locked in each other's arms, they defy death. Such termination leaves no sense of lack. The tragedy is complete, and the art which conceived such finale is nothing other than genius. George Eliot thrills us with a sense of power; and who but wishes to be gripped as if by some giant's hand upon the shoulder? You will find nothing commonplace about workman or work. Belonging to a brilliant era of romance, her star burns undimned. "Adam Bede," "Mill on the Floss," "Daniel Deronda," and "Romola" are instances of immortal fiction, and "Janet's Repentance" is a tale daintily and pathetically told.

On considering George Eliot's volumes, certain observations arise spontaneously. One is, Hers was a mind open to nature. Dickens and Thackeray gave slight heed to sky and field for their own sake. Clearly Eliot loved the fields and skies. "Mill on the Floss" is specially rich, I think, in tender sayings about out-of-doors. Not that this writer has touched hands with Blackmore; but that was not to be expected. There is but one "Lorna Doone."

Such passionate tenderness for nature comes to earth once only in many centuries. But in this authoress, constantly recurring, you shall find let drop words of love for the flow of a river, or tint of cloud, or gracious quiet of the evening, or hint of thinking where words are not articulated. Account this one strength in George Eliot.

And George Eliot has been declared best equipped of her contemporary novelists, and more the philosopher than Dickens or Thackeray. One thing is sure, she chose an ampler field than they. You can not designate her patrimony, as you can theirs. Dickens was biographer of slum and middle-class England; Thackeray biographer of aristocratic England; but you can not coin a phrase which shall express the territory pre-empted by George Eliot. But if her work-ground were less capable of defining than theirs, it does not follow she was profounder. Philosophy is not so much vocation as it is attribute. To be scholar it is not necessary to wear cap and gown, nor to be philosopher is it necessary to say, "I will philosophize." Who reads Thackeray must know that no acuter philosopher in character lived in his day. "Sartor Resartus" is not profounder philosphy than may be found in "Barry Lyndon" and "Vanity Fair." Eliot was equipped, but is no deeper nor can be nobler than may be found in "Sidney Carton" and "Henry Esmond." In her attempts we observe a girth of circumference which appeals to the mind. She was predisposed to framing systems. Order was omnipresent to her thought. Chaos turned to cosmos of some sort with her; for she was hostile to intellectual débris. In according her high rank in scope of plan and in quality of execution we may hasten to agree; but to make her outrank Thackeray and Dickens seems not to be warranted by the facts.

Another observation is, she has diversified her fields. Her flowers are not all planted in one soil. MacDonald and Black have one vein. We know where their next venture will land its cargo. This is not fortunate. The element of surprise should not absent itself from fiction. George Eliot saw this clearly. She made no two ventures on the same waters. The poor weaver, his pain, and pessimism and its cure,— this once, no more; and "Silas Marner," most graceful of her essays in fiction, does the heart good as songs of birds in the fields of spring.

"Middlemarch" and "Mill on the Floss" are well in the same field, but with emphasis on such diverse traits in character and society as practically to throw them into different worlds. In one the grief of mismating is the theme; in the other the harshness of character in father and son, and the sweet tenderness of a girl's life breaking through the one as a daisy through the sod. These fields were visited no more. She was no Ruth to glean in a harvested field, but rather as a traveler who pitches tent but once in any single spot, a camp-fire burnt to ashes, a memory, and away! "Adam Bede" dips pen into the woe of wrong. It is the drama of sin, with shame, sorrow, disaster, conscience. Not often has there been given a more graphic touch than when Hetty tells Dinah how she heard her deserted babe crying, even when she saw it was no longer where she had hidden it. Seth makes manliness seem a little taller; Dinah is a fair picture as we see her yet; Adam stands strong, a tower meant for defense; Mrs. Poyser's garrulity sounds in our ears to this hour; and the characters in "Mill on the Floss" stand out as painted by some master's brush—Tom Tulliver like his father, hard as flint; the mother an echo, but who, at the last, will let mother-love speak, and will go with Maggie into her undeserved disgrace; Philip, pure, manly, faithful, suffering, self-denying, unforgetting; Stephen, passionate in love as sweep of stormy sea,—who will forget them?

"Romola" leaves England and to-day, and migrates to Italy and history. This is George Eliot's attempt at writing the historical novel. Dickens wrote "Tale of Two Cities;" Thackeray, "Henry Esmond;" Eliot, "Romola;" and they are worthy of the era and the authors. This is the sole novel of our authoress which does not stay on English soil. Romola holds court in Italy. Lorenzo the Magnificent, Savonarola, Pico Mirandola, Romola, Tito Melema, are the actors, and each is worthy of prolonged study. The era is attractive. The historic currents in those days were widening in such fashion as had not been known since Rome died. Call it a brilliant and wicked age, and have done. It was flooded with the passion for scholarship characteristic of the Renaissance, discoveries awaking,—this the field; and in such field she has shown herself capable of satisfying the imagination and the historic and dramatic sense. "Romola" need not blush to stand in the presence of "Ivanhoe." Tito Melema is a great portrait. He is gibbeted forever. His versatile talent; his lack of moral stamina; his feeling his way toward crime as a bather into cold surf; his base ingratitude, and the choice of ambition rather than rightness; his fatal decision to make no search for his foster father, the appropriation of his wealth, and the consequent denial of him returned, and Melema's murder by that much injured man,—these constitute a study in ingratitude not often paralleled in power, and seldom equaled as a characterization. Becky Sharp and Tito Melema may make society for themselves, since they are members of an aristocracy in villainy seldom experienced.

In "Daniel Deronda" the scene is shifted to the Jew, that most fascinating race of history. That the author was saturated with Jewish history need not to be told any reader of this volume. Her step is of one who knows the path. Daniel Deronda is a rare creation, whether considered as a Jew or as a study in human kind. A pure and noble spirit is a generous contribution to literature; and such Deronda is. The unconscious power of him is magnetic, and to see how he guides Gwendolyn Harleth to her better womanhood is inspiring, though to watch her at his marriage and departure as she stands hungry-hearted and hungry-eyed has a pathos too deep for words. Viewing this work as a whole, let this be said: the departure was a success. This study of the Jew is of importance in contemporary fiction, in which the Jew is moving to such a chief place.

Another observation on Eliot is, her impersonality. She obscures her own views. This Thackeray and Dickens never did. They were always telling what they thought. George Eliot was an agnostic in philosophy, and a freelover in social ethics; but would anybody guess the one or the other from her novels? There is something singular here. In her romances marriage is nowhere indicted, but on the converse seems to be held in high esteem. There is a contradiction here. She would seem to have been malleable in opinion, subject to environing influences. George Henry Lewes discovered her to herself as novelist, and exercised a singular dominancy over her. His opinions in philosophy and social morality were hers; and whether she were conscious to herself of insincerity in her affected opinions, certain it is she nowhere intimates them in her novels. In poetry, she speaks in her own proper person; but with her fiction, the character elaborates itself, and speaks words native to itself. She does not use her creations as venders of her notions. I think George Eliot's work eminently impersonal; and the more I read, the more does this fact impress me. And this is a rare trait. It was Shakespeare's trait, though in him it arose from the many-sidedness of genius.

In George Eliot, to know to what this is attributable is not easy. Her philosophical self and her romancist self were two persons. In philosophical moods she was so cold as to deny life chance to bloom. Now if she was sure "the times were out of joint," then to her fell the task of setting right so far as in her lay. Wrong cries for righting, as all the reformers know. Now, to suppose George Eliot to have held at heart the views of her head, and not have apostled them, is to arraign her courage; and to question her honesty, is to arraign her sincerity. Such the Scylla and Charybdis one must pass in any criticism of her character and work. Ruskin tells his theories; to this end, as he supposed, was he born.

Matthew Arnold was an apostle of an outgrown aristocracy, misconceiving the shore on which he walked; and his poetry is apostle of his agnosticism, as Shelley's of his anarchy. Now is it conceivable that George Eliot truly held abberrant theories of marriage and theology, and did not attempt discipling the world? Between thought and heart there was some hiatus. At head she was agnostic; at heart, I take it, she was yearningly Christian. She could not advocate her barren faith when love lit her study-lamp. Therefore the impersonality of her views may be set down as indisposition to champion a system of thinking to which her heart gave no assent. She was distinctively religious in her natural symptoms. To doubt this would make the interpretation of Seth and Mordecai and the "Scenes from Clerical Life" impossible. A religious atmosphere suits her better moods. In intellectual theory, Buckle and Lewes and Eliot belonged to the same school. But recall the insistency of Buckle's advocacy of his materialistic theories, and the unhesitating teaching of Lewes; and the utter absence of such advocacy in Eliot's fiction more than implicative in spirit of championing opposite opinions;

and we can not refrain from believing she doubted the validity of her own intellectual attitude. Compare Mrs. Humphrey Ward, who has religious theories to vend in her shambling "Robert Elsmere." Here a resuscitated infidelity on the invalidity of the proof of miracles is donated a coat and hat and name; and the authoress supposes she has given a man. Mrs. Ward and George Eliot are of the same faith; how explain the latter's failure in indoctrination, save on the theory of her distrust of her religious conclusions? A discrepancy between the teaching of the head and of the heart is not an infrequent spectacle. George Eliot's example in social morality was unquestionably deleterious. The morality of marriage and its essentiality to our social system and order is too apparent to need defense. Heart and history testify in its behalf. To attack this system in example is a crime. George Eliot should have seen that while a phase of the marriage laws was a hurt to her individually, they were still a society safeguard and purity's necessity, while her marriage to Mr. Cross proves conclusively she might have found nuptial companionship with other than George Henry Lewes. As it was, she gave the weight of her conduct to a system to which she was in no true sense allied. That our attitude is often shaped by our self-wishes the instance of John Milton as related to divorce testifies. George Eliot was better than her theories would lead us to conclude, and her silences in her fictions are testimonies to her consciousness of incertitude and insincerity.

Viewing the author as related to her work, we must confess to a sense of lack. The large things she did, praise her; but the larger thing she might have done, upbraids her.

George Eliot's agnosticism is hopeless and pitiful. A woman without God is like a ship for which there is no sea. She seemed a vessel thrown on the high bar, to which no wave ever comes to bear it back into the deep. From this characteristic it follows that what may be named inspirational values were largely wanting in her. Inspiration implies a sky; and sky was what George Eliot always lacked. Her face was plain, her voice exceeding sweet, her genius commanding, her vision circumscribed, her hope dead; and so she leaves us with a sense of lack, as if we looked at an eagle tethered in a meadow. It was meant, as she was meant, for the mountain and the blue vault and the sun.

The Ring and the Book

"THE RING AND THE BOOK" is the most satisfactory poem ever written; which judgment this paper attempts to justify. The poem is a mediæval cathedral, and to be comprehended must be given both a general and a minute survey. We must estimate a cathedral's size, dignity, proportions, style of architecture, leap of spire, sense of sublimity, and hold this total impression, as a lake holds mountains mirrored. We weigh the mass, make a synthesis. We then proceed to the study of details. The spring of the arch, effect of aisle, nave, choir, transept, chapels; the windows, whose storied panes glorify the light; the organ, with sob of storm and soul, echoing along the pillars and dying in the arches; the solemn silence, more impressive than organ note,—these constitute an analysis; and by the dual survey we hold the cathedral a feudatory of the mind. "The Ring and the Book" is a Gothic cathedral, impressive and sublime. A general survey will reveal certain facts, among them these:

The book is epic in proportions, containing

twenty-one thousand verses. It is twice the length of "Paradise Lost," and six times as long as "Hamlet," one-sixth longer than Homer's "Iliad," and a third longer than Dante's "Inferno." It is greater than the bulk of many a great poet's works. Its wealth of thought, eloquence, loveliness of diction, profound soul-scrutiny, fertility of imagination, mastery of the resources of poetry, pregnant utterance, high ideality, are fitted to immortality as finger to the lute. The book is very long, but none too long when studied and loved. Its epic length is due to its epic mass of thought. An ocean's flood requires an ocean's bed. Compare "The Ring and the Book" with Spenser's "Fairie Queen," and discover striking similarities. Both are pure in moral tone as mountain air; both are mediæval in location and temper; both catch the spirit of knight errantry; both are dedicated to holiest uses, the illumination of the understanding, and the purifying of the heart; both delight us like the songs of birds at dawn; and the authors of both are poets such as literature has had few of. The "Fairie Queen" is an allegory; "The Ring and the Book" a history. One is descriptive; the other analytical.

I read "The Fairie Queen" with growing passion. Edmund Spenser is England's noblest troubadour, and, aside from Tennyson, most musical of English poets. It were a sign of literary health if at this fountain, youth would drink as at mountain springs. Spenser charms as the sound of rain upon the roof at night, and is grateful to the weary thought as the house of sleep which himself has described with such dreamy imagination and perfect melody:

"And more to lulle him in his slumber soft
   A trickling streame from high rock tumbling downe,
And ever-drizzling raine upon the loft,
   Mixt with a murmuring winde, much like the sowne
   Of swarming bees, did cast him in a swowne.
No other noyse, nor people's troublous cryes,
   As still are wont t' annoy the walled towne,
Might there be heard; but careless quiet lyes
Wrapt in eternal silence farre from enemyes."

But comparison will leave the crown on Browning. His is the philosopher's art set to the music of poetry. His thought cuts deep like a crusader's sword. He digs into the soul, and lets it bleed. All realms of recent thinking, hemispheres unknown to Spenser, are put under tribute. All are his vassals. He pours forth light as the sun. The history in "The Ring and the Book" is mediæval, but the thought is modern as this noon. Browning's is an amplitude of genius Spenser did not possess. To an epic narrative he has superadded a dramatic penetration. Spenser is more melodious than Browning; and Browning is more profound than Spenser.

"The Ring and the Book" is Browning's masterpiece, sustaining the same relation to his multitudinous poems as Hamlet to Shakespeare's remaining dramas. "Colombe's Birthday," "Blot in the 'Scutcheon," and "Pippa Passes" are usually acorded rank in point of finish, delicacy, and dramatic perfection; but they are brief. They are half-hours of sunshine; "The Ring and the Book" is a day. Comparison between an author's own efforts is never absolutely just. Every man has his best. Power is not steady. Browning's variety of theme and breadth of treatment afford ample opportunity for comparison and criticism. He is the most unequal of poets. And then, too, the personality in readers is so diverse. Moods change an emphasis of appreciation, as sky the color of the sea. Ourselves are a variable quantity. The subjective in the reader will be as influential an element in choice of a favorite poem as the objective in the writer. In criticism, critics can not get on the same ground. To a lover, his love's voice will be the sweetest of voices; and why quarrel with him? To ask a company which of an author's poems each prefers is stimulative, since there is thus disclosed this individuality in choice to which reference is here made. Browning's lesser dramas are beautiful, but brief. They are snatches of music sung by happy hearts on happy days; but "The Ring and the Book" is an oratorio. They are dedicated to bringing a single thought from bud to bloom. In "Pippa Passes" that thought is Conscience regnant; in "Blot in the 'Scutcheon," tarnished virtue has in itself no more a remedy within itself to recall its lost self than a faded flower to recover its vanished loveliness; in "Colombe's Birthday," the triumph of love in a good woman's heart. In "The Ring and the Book" these themes are amalgamated as grains of gold to form a ring for love to wear upon its finger. The weightiest questions of life are discussed, and in such satisfactory fashion as makes it the most adequate poem of literature. An epic in twelve books, a tragedy in a single act! For my part, I feel with this massive poem as I do in watching Niagara, a grave, laughterless delight. Smiles vanish from the face in looking on Niagara, or reading "The Ring and the Book."

And "The Ring and the Book" is unique. Poetry has not its like. It stands solitary, as a forsaken soldier. What poem do you recall resembling this in the least? The tragedies of Æschylus, Sophocles, Shakespeare, Goethe, have set no fashion for it. Contrast any dramas these authors have written with the poem discussed, and this uniqueness will strike you with sudden joy. In Æschylus's "Prometheus Bound," you are confronted with continuity in action and progress in movement. Characters rise, speak, pass, or, if reintroduced, their coming marks the lapse of time. Moments have swept them on as to a new stage. Prometheus is chained to his crag, and the crag is buckled to the world; but that world has moved. While we have listened to Prometheus, Kratos, and the Oceanides, he has drawn a trifle nearer the end of his pain.

We are conscious of progress toward conclusion. In Sophocles's "Antigone," the same is true. Antigone goes toward her doom, sometimes with bowed head and hindered step and slow; sometimes driving swiftly as if running a race toward death, but always motion. There is neither stagnation nor yet movement in circles, but progress evident as day. In "Faust" is perennial action. Mephistopheles, Faust, Margaret,—cynical diabolism in Mephistopheles; in the others, ambition, love, temptation, yielding, sin, retribution,—love and conscience in Margaret, and selling of soul and remorse terrible and useless in Faust, but action, always action! Characters run toward their doom. Fever is in the tragedy's pulse. We feel as certain events rush toward a tragic termination, as Niagara's rapids toward a precipice. Let King Lear speak for Shakespeare's method. Events tend toward a crisis. The drift of seas past a headland is not more, or so apparent. Goneril and Regan and Edmund; Cordelia and King Lear, old and abdicating his throne; his misjudgment of Cordelia, coupled with cruel thoughts and words; he is despised of his daughters; he gradually comes to himself, state and power gone as certainly as color fades from evening cloud; his anguish at heart; his finding in Cordelia more than he had lost in kingdom; his gray, blind despair when on the stormy moor with disheveled locks he walks a madman, and at the last bearing his dead Cordelia in his arms, his life the passion of sob, he dies,—these are currents swift as swollen mountain torrent. In all, we find as definite motion as when a ship sails along a coast, and sees the headlands slipping behind like drifting fisher's boats.

In "The Ring and the Book" the plan is diametrically diverse. There is no movement. All the story is told in the first thousand verses; and twenty thousand verses are consumed in rehearsing a tale once told. If there be such another production in literature, I do not know of it. In plot, "The Ring and the Book" is absolutely unique.

A closing observation on the work, as a whole, is that all Browning's characteristics riot here. He is as a herald who, having flung aside all weights, runs his solitary race, a nude personality. Here see his versatility, intellectuality, dramatic instinct, and originality. That a poet could so variegate a single story as to tell it over nine times, and it not weary you, is sufficient proof of versatility. To this add the exactitude with which he develops natures so variant as those of Count Guido, Caponsacchi, Pompilia, and the Pope, and wonder blinds us, as looking full in the sun's face. His intellectuality is evidenced in his grasp on the strategic nature of the story; in his penetration into motive; in his profound disquisition on contemporary social questions; in his practically illimitable command of apt, pertinent, luminous, and beautifully poetical illustration; in the serene sky he keeps, nothing bewildered by the jungle growth of interacting motives and complications of argument. Dramatic here, as always, Browning has written the longest drama in literature. Each actor speaks his part, then leaves the stage. But his very story is dramatic, and suggests a stage with many players. You, by Browning's subtle power of suggestion, hear a dialogue where none is spoken. His dramatic impulse guides Browning unerringly, as instinct the sea-fowl along "his solitary way." I call this power masterfully dramatic. No one questions his originality. There is nobody like him. No one could think him a borrower. Bayne and Stedman may discuss

Tennyson's debt to Theocritus; but to whom is Browning debtor? Lender he is, not borrower. He is opulent in originality. His themes are new as unexplored seas. This trait is observable in all Browning's poetry; but in no place so noticeable as in "The Ring and the Book." The audacity of the undertaking is a delight; but the consummate genius exhibited in execution is a larger delight. To tell all one had to tell in a prelude, and ask readers to stay twenty thousand verses longer? Nothing more original has ever been conceived than this poem. And when we consider how he came last of our great poets, when each had harvested and gleaned the field, and that we are so impressed with the originality of no poet since Homer, wonder grows.

Now to the special survey of this mediæval cathedral: Astronomers who would watch a transit of Venus go half about the world to find a spot for planting their telescope. We dare not be less wise in watching the transit of a soul. Catch the movement of the central sun, and the movements of all planets will become apparent. And Pompilia is central sun of "The Ring and the Book." She is the *dramatis persona.* In the light of her character all else becomes visible. Woman's centrality in the drama of life is thus expressed. Count Guido the husband, and Caponsacchi, priest, deliverer and lover, are chief foils; while Pietro and Violante, professed father and mother of Pompilia, one half, and the other half Rome, the deliberate judgment of Rome, lawyers, and gray, pure Pope, are ancillary merely.

The geography of these twelve books is, prelude stating data of the tragedy, opinion of Rome sympathetic toward Guido, followed by opinion sympathetic toward Pompilia, closing with the deliberate judgment of those capable of coming to a wise conclusion in view of all the evidence; then Count Guido, fresh from the rack, tells his story; after him Caponsacchi, with news of Pompilia's murder at the hands of Guido and his confederates freshly come to him; then Pompilia, lying wounded, white, faint, dying, breathes out her story tender as a tale of hapless love, pleas of prosecution and defense filled brimful of scholastic subtleties, the Pope soliloquizes in words of beauty, pathos, depth, and discernment; and on his last night on earth, Guido, in presence of cardinal and abate, speaks once more, and, as before, utters only lies, until his last word, when one truth is spoken, then our poet's postlude; and "The Ring and the Book" is ended. Such the scaffolding of this poem.

The crime of marriage for position is theme of "The Ring and the Book," and we are in the midst of a grave social question. Marriage is the basis of society. Roman Catholicism says, Marriage is a sacrament; the State says, Marriage is a civil contract; atheism says, Marriage is slavery; Protestantism says, Marriage is a divine institution, implying a union of souls solemnized by a religious ceremony; and God says, Marriage is a necessity of civilization and righteousness. Marriage, what shall we do with it? is a current problem. Grant Allen and Hardy say, Abolish it. George Eliot and George Henry Lewes say, Abolish it. Marriage is a living theme; and most profound of all discussions of this vital topic is "The Ring and the Book." Browning has given two discussions of marriage; one in James Lee's wife, the other in Pompilia. The former is a sweet woman, loving her husband, and waking up to the sad truth which clouds her life like autumn afternoon. She is outside her husband's world. He does not think of her. She is no necessary part of his heart's furnishing. And she is lonely, bereft, a widow without widow's weeds,—a widow, and no grave on which she may plant flowers and rain her tears. She is going away from him, hopelessly, loving him still, longing for him; and could she hear his voice crying, "Come back, my love," her heart would leap with joy. But no recalling voice is heard, and she sails away, lonely and alone.

"The Ring and the Book" is a study in marriage for position—the barter of a woman for a count's coat-of-arms. The exchange of wealth for ancestry, how recent this sale sounds! Is it of Pompilia this story speaks? Surely we had been able to supply another name not so entirely unfamiliar to our ears. And if crime ever received terrible arraignment, marriage for position has received that arraignment from Robert Browning. "The Ring and the Book" is the tragedy of marriage not for love, but for place. The story is: Pompilia, a child of thirteen, beloved, pure, beautiful, and rich, is by her mother's mistaken love espoused and wedded to a nobleman for his name. He is an aristocrat, vile, past life's prime, very poor, and trades his blood for gold. Violante meant her matchmaking in love. She longed to see Pompilia, her beloved, happy and great; as if anything could compensate for lack of love! Strange a mother should know no better. She meant to make her daughter happy as singing birds, and did make her more miserable than words know how to tell, and became in effect her murderer. Pompilia was child in years, but more a child in thought. She knew nothing of marriage beyond the name. She was simple as a flower, and happy as the birds in dewy dawns. Care floated no cloud across her sky. All was love and laughter; but a priest, brother to Count Guido, saw how he might recover his brother's lost fortune and his own, and with simple Violante plans this union between his brother and her daughter; and Violante, without the knowledge of Pietro, takes Pompilia to a cathedral in the hush of a rainy evening, and weds her to Count Guido. The wedding done, Pompilia is left alone, and thinks the matter ended. But Guido claims his wife. Pietro objects and yields, he and Violante going to the count's villa at Arrezzo, to be near their child, who is sunshine to their age. Guido hates this child-wife, and, with machinations base as Iago's plottings, schemes to rid him of his wife, but become possessor of her gold; for he had wed gold, and not woman. He succeeds in driving father and mother away, and then exercises all his diabolical cunning to drive his wife into imprudence. He places her in the theater so her beauty may be observed; writes madrigals with his own hand, affecting they come from an enamored priest, writing this priest letters of passionate love to which Pompilia's name is attached; persecutes her with the presence and advices of a maid, Guido's paramour; makes her estate worse than death. She longs to die, seeks help from confessor, then a bishop; is made sport of, is rebuffed; prays still with breaking heart, and at last suffers as one benumbed, careless for life, but eager if eagerness knows her face, for death. Then in the drowse of this lethargy, she finds herself keeper of a life other than hers, God's promise of a babe; then, then only, she appeals to Caponsacchi to lend his help. He answers, "I am yours." They escape, are overtaken by Guido, who has plotted for this; Pompilia is not restored to him by the Church, her babe is born; then, since the babe is Guido's, and through it he may inherit the mother's fortune, he murders Violante, Pietro, and Pompilia, is captured, tried, condemned, beheaded; and his poison blood leaks through the scaffold planks. So

"Let this old woe step on the stage once more."

Pompilia is the fairest portrait of woman put on canvas by any artist to this hour. A bud not yet become a flower, a sunbeam glinting on a stream, no more! when suddenly her life meets scourge and fire like martyr at the stake; passes through flame, and comes forth with not the smell of fire upon it; meets life's fearful problems; lives tragedy through to its bloody goal; struggles with every shape of shame which courts a soul, and comes through all spotless as unflecked clouds that float across the roof of heaven. Concerning her, hear the Pope say:

"First of the first,
Such I pronounce Pompilia, then as now
Perfect in whiteness."

"At least one blossom makes me proud at eve,
Born mid the briers of my inclosure."

"My flower,
My rose, I gather for the breast of God."

Pompilia represents triumph over heredity. The nameless daughter of a shameless mother makes a world debtor for her gracious life. Guido had heredity for a help. Pope Innocent was right in saying concerning him:

"I find him bound then, to begin life well;
  Fortified by propitious circumstance,
  Great birth, good breeding, with the Church for
    guide,
  How lives he? Cased thus in a coat of proof,
  Mailed like a man-at-arms, though all the while
  A puny starveling."

Of Count Guido much might in reason have been prophesied; but he is less than man. He shames the race that bore him. He was a parasite on society. Not one poor nobility blesses his life; he did not even know how to die. Cowards do often, while pallor whitens cheek and lip, yet gather up their little manliness to die. But Guido died coward as he lived, a shriek upon his lips. So base a soul has not often been conceived. His face and figure are limned with rarest art. He is man at his worst. Iago was not so vile as he; for Iago plotted against Othello's wife; Guido plotted against his own. He comes fresh from the rack with a lie upon his lips. He affects to have been injured:

"This getting tortured merely in the flesh
  Amounts to almost an agreeable change.
  Four years have I been operated on
  I, the soul, do you see—its tense and tremulous part—

My self-respect, my care for a good name
  Pride in an old one, love of kindred—just
  A mother, brothers, sisters, and the like,
  That looked up to my face when the days were dim,
  And fancied they found light there—no one spot,
  Foppishly sensitive, but has paid its pang."

Huger hypocrisy does not breathe. The rack, he says, was tenderness matched with his hurt. With swollen joint and shoulder sprung from socket, with obsequious looks and words, he attempts ogling this court, and besmirching Pompilia. He has murdered her; now he will murder her good name, the solitary good he has not already bereft her of. With consummate skill he makes covert appeal to every prejudice lying hid at the jurors' hearts, his noble house, his priestly apprenticeship, the slumbering hatred of patrician for plebeian; he forgets no one of them. The rack has quickened all his intellectual powers until his mediocre capacity stands him for genius. He is fighting a battle for life. That calls his mightiest forth. When he is done, you loathe him as you do a serpent, only more, seeing he has made himself so venomous and slimy. You can not name a virtue in him. God saw none.

An old libertine covetous for gold. He will steal from his own child, and he a two-weeks' babe! He wedded a child for gold. He saw she was simple and pure. The sight of her helplessness might have turned a flint to tenderness. It touched not Guido. He hounds her with a pertinacity and diabolism which would have shamed Iago. Every snare a foul mind could conceive, he set. He calls a harlot to his help to trip his wife. She was hunted!

The look upon her face would make marble weep; he did only redouble diligence to snare her, finding no fault in her. A serpent charming a singing-bird unto its death is too fair a figure for this man. He is despicably mean. His vices are the very depravity of vice.

"Not one permissible impulse moves the man,
From the mere liking of the eye and ear,
To the true longing of the heart that loves,—
No trace of these; but all to instigate
Is what sinks man past level of the brute."

"All is lust for money; to get gold,—
Why lie, rob; if it must be, murder!"

"Always subordinating (note the point!)
Revenge, the manlier sin, to interest,
The meaner."

And

"Those letters false beyond all forgery."

His hypocrisy clings to him close as skin to flesh. On that night preluding his execution, you may hear his

"O, that men would be good!"

He is the Pharisee by trade. His life is one long villainy. He had no better moments. He had so acclimated his soul to shame as to be steeped in it. He did not pray, seeing he was practical atheist. God was not, for he called nature God. God was no factor in his life. He had been afforded training by the Church. His was no lack of opportunity. His light was sufficient. He sinned against abundant knowledge. He was sterile of virtue, as a bleak rock of plant and soil. His life had been a lie; his testimony fresh come from the rack's twinge, and in death-chamber waiting the scaffold, was one reverberated perjury. One splinter of truth was struck from him as he stumbled to the scaffold, as lightning breaks splinters from the rock. Pope Innocent soliloquizes:

"For the main criminal I have no hope
   Except in such a suddenness of fate.
   I stood at Naples once, a night so dark
   I could have scarce conjectured there was earth
   Anywhere, sky or sea or world at all;
   But the night's black was burst through by a
      blaze—
   Thunder struck blow on blow, earth groaned and
      bore,
   Through her whole length of mountain visible;
   There lay the city thick and plain with spires,
   And, like a ghost, disshrouded, white the sea.
   So may the truth be flashed out by one blow,
   And Guido see one instant, and be saved."

Then hear Guido shriek:

"Who are these you have let descend my stair?
Ha, their accursed psalm! Lights at the sill!
Is it 'Open' they dare bid you? Treachery!
Sirs, have I spoken one word all this while
Out of the world of words I had to say?
Not one word! All was folly—I laughed and mocked!
Sirs, my first true word, all truth and no lie,
Is, save me notwithstanding! Life is all!
I was just stark mad,—let the madman live,
Pressed by as many chains as you please to pile!
Do n't open! Hold me from them! I am yours;
I am the grandduke's—no, I am the Pope's!
Abate, Cardinal, Christ, Maria, God,
Pompilia, will you let them murder me?"

And a scaffold wet with blood, villain's blood; and Count Guido Franceschina is the voice of a curse lingering in the air! What a consummate work of genius is this portraiture! Such was the scion of a noble house, a man of ancestry and inspiring environment.

But Pompilia, of whom nothing could be expected, seeing heredity was so foul, Pompilia lived a life lovely as any dream of God. That is life. We are not creatures, but creators. God and a soul are competent to triumph over heredity. But Pompilia is alone. All are against her. Her mother sold her as a babe. Husband, maid, Church, are her foes. She has no love, no memory of one bright day, immortal as the heart. Know you anybody so alone as she? Chaucer's Griselda was upholden by the memory that her wedded love had been so beautiful while it was hers. Enid could not forget her husband had loved her utterly upon a day. Desdemona had Emilia for as fast a friend as ever championed a cause. She had Iago; but she had Othello, too. She was sure he loved her, and never surer than when at his hands she died. His murder was certificate of his love. But Pompilia had nobody. She was so alone! Maid traitor to her, and seeking her ruin, Guido never loved her, and indifference was kindled into hate. Alone! Poor Pompilia! *Poor* Pompilia! When Gwendolyn Grandcourt felt her better self going from her, Daniel Deronda was her stay. Pompilia was utterly alone. No human sympathy touches her. She was bereft—but she had God! This is the secret of her purity and triumph. Fighting this fight for truth, she felt for God. And as her days gloomed blacker than night, and she found life all but dragged from its moorings, God was all her help. Guido was atheist; Pompilia was stout to hold to God. She groped, God seemed so far removed, poor child!—so far removed, and seemed to hide his face. Then Pompilia reached hands high in the darkness, and on a sudden, when hope felt like a breaking staff, she caught the hand of the Eternal Strength. She prayed; that saved her. Betrayed of man, she held to God, and he did not betray her; but brought her through deep waters in safety unto heaven.

One day there was turned a page of life on which suffering was not written. At the play, whither Guido had taken her to snare her, sitting in the gallery, where he had seated her, himself invisible, she saw the sad and noble face of Caponsacchi. He was looking at her as a watcher at the stars, and saw a face of surprising beauty, but of unutterable sadness. Laughter knew not how to run across that face, once the home of joy. And sight of this man's face made it possible for Pompilia to know great love before death brought silence. And Caponsacchi was only less noble in manhood than Pompilia in womanhood. Literature must wander far before another such poem as Caponsacchi's narrative shall be told. He was priest and man; and what more could praise utter? He saw and loved, and beneath her lattice he watched, suspicioning she might have need of him,—watched with such large fidelity as love uses at a bed of pain. Guido wrote letters to him purporting to come from Pompilia; but this lover was not deceived. He trusted the face he had seen, and felt confirmed in his belief she could not be of such a sort. She sent him no word nor gave him any look, but her sad face haunted him. If she drew near a casement and saw him, she slipped back into darkness. Truth was in him and penetration. He was writer of poems for the bishop's need. He was a man through all, nor molded to be a court puppet. He haunted lattice and street as whip-poor-wills do the woods at night. Her unutterable sadness makes mute appeal to him, and is graven on his memory as by graver's sharpest tool. At last Pompilia, in extremity of distress, appeals to his chivalry. He knows he risks all in helping; but no danger was hazard if he might bring her succor. The love for remote stars had not been purer than his love for her. He planned the escape, was censured of his order, was laughed at as if his had been a youthful escapade. They reckoned him among themselves; for knighthood like his they could not conceive, he being as remote from them as if he had been full citizen of heaven. His was that large self-forgetfulness in which love takes delight. He sees need, duty; what need he more? Innocent looking on him with tears' dim mists in his eyes, whispers,

> "Thou, pledged to dance not fight
> Sprang'st forth the hero!"

Let his self-forgetfulness gleam out like fires from precious stones in this:

> "For Pompilia, be advised.
> Build churches, go pray! You will find me there,
> I know, if you come—and you will come I know.
> Why, there's a Judge weeping! Did I not say
> You were good and true at bottom? You see the
>   truth—
> I am glad I helped you: she helped me just so."

And Pope Innocent:

> "Thou whose sword-hand was used to strike the lute,
> Whose sentry-station graced some wanton's gate,
> Thou did'st push forward and show mettle, shame
> The laggards, and retrieve the day. Well done!
> Be glad thou hast let light into the world,

> Through that irregular breach o' the boundary,—
> see
> The same upon thy path and march assured,
> Learning anew the use of soldiership,
> Self-abnegation, freedom from all fear,
> Loyalty to the life's end!"

And such manhood had serene rewards. He was held in Pompilia's heart as any saint. It was worth all it cost, and more. She says:

> "'T is now when I am most upon the move
> I feel for what I verily find—again
> The face, again the eyes, again through all,
> The heart and its immeasurable love
> Of my one friend, my only, all my own,
> Who put his breast between the spears and me.
> Ever with Caponsacchi! Otherwise,
> Here alone would be failure, loss to me—
> How much more loss to him, with life debarred
> From giving life, love locked from love's display,
> The day-star stopped its task that makes night
> morn!
> O lover of my life, O soldier-saint,
> No work begun shall ever pause for death!
> Love will be helpful to me more and more
> I' the coming course, the new path I must tread—
> My weak hand in thy strong hand, strong for
> that!
> Tell him that if I seem without him now,
> That 's the world's insight. O, he understands!

He is at Civita—do I once doubt
The world again is holding us apart?
He had been here, displayed in my behalf
The broad brow that reverberates the truth,
And flashed the word God gave him back to man!"

To reflect God, that is life's goal; and to have lived a life at whatever cost which leaves such impress, would turn the gall it drank to wine, and change gloom to glory. And this lover came to teach her love. He came into a barren heart bereft of all, and sorely needing help and love. God was her stay, but love like his illumines God. It is not hard to hold that God is love, when once we know some woman or some man is love.

Only when Pompilia finds herself a promised mother, does she plan to flee. Her life might die; she could be glad for that; but now she is not her own. Another life holds her skirts. She throws herself on Caponsacchi, crying, "Help, O help!" They flee. The story hastes. Her babe is born. Guido comes to the door of her father's home, and it is Christmas time! He whispers, "Caponsacchi!" whereat the door is opened—then murder thrusts and slays Pietro, Violante, Pompilia. She lives to tell her story. God was good to her in this. To tell her woe as she lies, white, weak, dying,—this is Pompilia's vindication, if she needed one. Truth sits upon her dying lips, as on her living lips. To hear this dying story is to listen to an angel speak. She utters no recriminatory words. No bitterness mixes with her speech. Upon her ears the music of her morning breaks. In sight and sound of heaven she falters forth her story, tells it so that help high as mountains lifts us toward God. She has no words of blame; rather words of palliation. Nor is she conscious of this merit. She blames not her mother, who bore her in shame and sold her:

"If she sold . . . what they call sold . . . me her child,
I shall believe she hoped in her poor heart
That I at least might try be good and pure,
Begin to live untempted, not go doomed
And done with ere once found in fault as she."

In behalf of Violante, she whispers,

"Do let me speak for her you blame so much."

"Yes, everybody that leaves life sees all
Softened and bettered; so with other sights;
To me, at least, was never evening yet
But seemed far beautifuler than its day,
For past is past."

And for Guido, the reef on which her life was wrecked—for Guido, her murderer, she has forgiveness:

> "For that most woeful man, my husband once,
> Who, needing respite, still draws vital breath,
> I—pardon him? So far as lies in me,
> I give him for his good the life he takes,
> Praying the world will therefore acquiesce.
> Let him make God amends!"

Since in God's face

> "Is light, but in his shadow healing too;
> Let Guido touch the shadow and be healed!"

Caponsacchi must not grieve as though in him were blame:

> "Say, from the deed no touch
> Of harm came, but all good, all happiness,
> Not one faint fleck of failure."

"This one heart gave me all the spring."

And Pompilia died, a woman of only seventeen years! Yet she had lived life through. The Pope saw that. He was one clean, strong man grown gray. How he saw virtue shine! How undimmed his sight for seeing goodness. Naught escaped him there. No fog hung on this landscape. His monologue is beautiful as a psalm sung in the evening's twilight. "This gray, ultimate decrepitude" sees Guido, Caponsacchi, and Pompilia as seen of God. In matters moral, his sight is keen as eagle's; and Innocent knew Pompilia had lived a life whose girth outspanned this dull world. She had loved. Great love swept round her like a sea. She had known motherhood, God's delight for woman:

"They loved me as I love my babe
(—Nearly so, that is—quite so could not be—)"

"Then I must lay my babe away with God,
Nor think of him again for gratitude."

"Till my boy was born,
Born all in love, with naught to spoil the bliss
A whole long fortnight; in a life like mine
A fortnight filled with bliss is long and much.
All women are not mothers of a boy,
Though they live twice the length of my whole life,
And, as they fancy, happily all the same."

She had met evil, and had triumphed and grown strong:

"Was the trial sore?
Temptation sharp? Thank God a second time!
Why comes temptation but for man to meet
And master, and make crouch beneath his foot
And so be pedestaled in triumph?"

"So my heart be struck,
What care I, by God's gloved hand or the bare?
Nor do I much perplex me with aught hard,
Dubious in the transmitting of the tale;
No, nor with certain riddles set to solve.
This life is training and a passage: pass—
Still, we march over some flat obstacle
We made give way before us: solid truth
In front of it, what motion for the world?
The moral sense grows but by exercise.
'T is even as a man grew probatively
Initiated in Godship, set to make
A fairer moral world than this he finds,
Guess now what shall be known hereafter."

And well for her. She had conquered.

"Life is probation, and the earth no goal
But starting-point of man."

And she has begun so nobly! The storm was terrible, but Pompilia has come through unscathed. Nay, the very storm has cleared her sky of vapors, and she saw to the dim outposts of the world, and beheld God, her lover never failing. Life was brief indeed, but long enough to get hold on God; and that is life at its best.

"For I trust
In the compensating, great God."

"So what I hold by is my prayer to God."

And God did not forget her! How blessed that is! She had found God the mighty. She and Christ were nearer than earth can ever bring two hearts. She had learned that duty was larger than earthly love. The tragedy of divided love is not so pathetic as the tragedy of duty foresworn for love. Love and duty, both met! And how she loves! I know not any poetry more deep in its sad music than the closing of Pompilia's story. Her voice grows weak and eyes grow dim, and since she can not hold Caponsacchi's hand in passing into silence, her heart reverts to him:

> "Tell him
> It was the name of him I sprang to meet
> When came the knock, the summons, and the end.
> 'My great heart, my strong hand are back again!'
> I would have sprung to these beckoning across
> Murder and hell gigantic and distinct
> O' the threshold, posted to exclude me heaven;
> He is ordained to call, and I to come!
> . . . .
> So let him wait God's instant men call years;
> Meantime hold hard by truth and his great soul,
> Do out the duty! Through such souls alone
> God, stooping, shows sufficient of his light
> For us i' the dark to rise by. And I rise."

And now her attempted word sinks low to whisper, and her whisper no mortal ear can catch, a quiver of the lids, a quick, glad smile as if in going she had met a friend she loved—and Pompilia is

> "Passed
> To where beyond these voices there is peace."

She has conquered heredity, environment, shameless duplicity, and found how God would keep them who trusted in him. And death came? What of that? She had lived life, had seen God with naked eyeball. And death was no more than a stepping across a runnel far among the hills, a step—and then—the blue of distant mountains, the shifting shadows of the clouds, the voice of waters, the infinite blue, and—the deathless morning and the face of God!

Shylock and David as Interpreters of Life

A SURFACE difference between marble and flesh is one of color. Flesh has color; marble is colorless. And this may be set down as an unvarying truth, life is always tinted, borrowing pigments from within and without. A sea has color of its own. Mid-Atlantic's blues are ravishing; but whoever has sailed the seas, knows their color is a variable quantity. They do not hold their own tenaciously. A sea with inherent hues still borrows colors from the clouds. I have seen oceans gray as dawn, dreary as winter clouds, silver as moonlight, crimson as heroes' blood, murky as rainy twilights, black as storm. This is a commonplace of the seas; they have been colored by the skies. In this regard character is not infrequently like the seas. Environment may color it. Similarity ends here; for seas have no choice, since skies are their masters. But character determines color for itself. The moment we approach character, necessity is an obsolete word. Character is shapable truly; but is more truly originative and shaping. Oceans are results; characters are causes.

In two dramas, "The Merchant of Venice" and "Saul," Shakespeare and Browning have offered estimates of life. Consider how Shylock sees the world, and how David sees the world. And the world is a stable quantity. An enumeration of qualities is possible. Some things our world is; some things our world is not. Idealism is not a sincere philosophy. Man does not create a world by thought. He is inhabitant, not creator. Earth is no objectified thought. Kant and Plato misled us. They trifled with our consciousness. Thought feels a world is dual, not singular. Self and non-self make up the category of existence. The world is certain, as solid. Reid's philosophy holds. Man is right. Could man take inventory of this planet's stock, he might, the inventory ended, say, "This is your world." How, then, shall we account for the variant views men hold of life? How explain men's seeing a different world? Does not the idealist seem right? To one man the earth is a witch's caldron, a receptacle of filth; to another, a theater for sublime activities. What, then, are there two worlds; or is each an objectification of individual thought? No! Neither view is correct. There is one world, real, substantial, gripped of gravitation, and lighted by the sun. Both men were accurate of vision. What both saw was there. Earth is a caldron boiling to the rim with shame; earth is a theater for heroisms; and who sees the whole world sees this. A profound philosophy eliminates neither factor, sees both, catalogues both. Earth is a totality. Light

"Fires the proud tops of the eastern pines;"

but darkness, too, has silent and solemn pomp, and exercises sovereignty through many a midnight. What boots it to deny self-evident truths? An entire world is a true world. Man sees a segment, and names his petty section all. A valley shut in of solemn mountains is a poem, but is not the earth. Who named it so, misnamed it. What is needed is a complete philosphy. A solitary hemisphere needs a new world to fill out its lacking bulk. Ruskin saw other world than Carlyle saw. The cosmos each saw was real enough. The actual world was what both saw. Therefore we may set this down as truth, The world is all we see. The fallacy is, man insists his narrow horizon includes the world. The value of Shylock and David as exponents is that they stand at opposite poles. Shylock was pessimist; David was optimist.

A man has dual value, as a person and as a representative. Who sees Shylock and David, sons of one race, will look again. Shylock with his furrowed face, his beetling brows, his eyes flashing like dagger's points, his cruel setting of the lips boding no pity, his face from which laughter has died out so long ago you can not realize sunlight ever brightened the somber landscape, tangled and disheveled locks threaded with silver, evident force on face and form,—this is Shylock. David is a youth. The joy of morning brightens on him, and the voice of morning sings in him. His cheek is ruddy, his locks are tangled gold. The odors of the Bethlehem hills still scent his garments, genius lights his eyes like Oriental dawns, a poet's touch twangs the harp he holds, dreams waken where he comes, and his fingers which

"Glimpsed down the strings of his harp
In a tremulous refrain,"

have a prophecy of might to grip a sword or scepter,—this is David. And Shylock is talking of restitution, and David is talking of restoration. Shylock there is self; David there is Saul. Shylock is pessimist; David is optimist.

Timon of Athens is Shakespeare's conscious pessimist, Lear and Shylock his unconscious pessimists. Timon despises and curses. Shylock, seeing his hour, seizes it and demands. Timon is words; Shylock is deeds. Two interpretations of Shylock obtain. Shylock is base, revengeful, shameless, crammed with causeless hate, holding ducats above daughter,—is, in short, the sum of villainies; or Shylock is a wronged race, hated, spit upon, used as men use tongs to handle coals, a man sinned against rather than sinning, a noble self-respect, an outraged spirit, might grown cruel through persecution, his hate justifiable resentfulness; Shylock needs condoning, merits sympathy. Adopt which view you will, he is *the person* of the comedy. His is the strong spirit of the play. Whom will you match with him? Surely not Bassanio nor Antonio; not Portia nor Lorenzo nor Jessica. We could not compare him with the duke of Venice nor the princes of Morocco and Aragon. Bassanio is singularly lacking in color. Character is not catalogued in his possessions. Antonio excites our surface sympathy. We see him at his best. Friendship gets him in danger of his death. He is pictured as the compassionate and injured gentleman, and we sob, "Poor, poor Antonio!" but have in reason been spectators of the one heroism of his life. And this nobility colors all our interpretation of him. But of anticipated heroism there seems no intimation. Strength was no possession of his soul. His hand on ours does not make us thrill as to the touch of love. 'T is lesser manhood we behold in him. We see it as a flashlight view. The overbearing merchant is shown us by indignant Shylock. Let us conclude, Antonio is no man to hold our admiration. He does not bear acquaintance. His nobility, like dew on flowers, disappears as day progresses. Lorenzo is a lover consummate in the art of making love. Poetry clings to his words. Moonlight and music conspire to glorify him. His voice is sweet as winds whispering in the pines. The whole world loves a lover, therefore is Lorenzo safe, but stands on no merit save that he is a lover. Jessica is much besides ideal. She is blind love, no more. That she would flee and filch is scarcely to her credit. But Portia? She is Shakespeare's "intellectual woman!" Portia is a woman. Her heart pleads. Her turning of the bond against Shylock is not law, but a trick; a poor subterfuge, with no semblance of law upon it; feminine alertness, not legal sagacity. Nothing about Portia argues intellectuality. As a woman in love she is charming, as what woman is not?

Shylock, if these estimates be even proximately true, has no fellow in the play. We can not ignore him. Strength, cunning, penetration, remembrance of wrong, iron determination,—these are patent in Shylock. He is a Jew, and loves money and is genius in its acquisition; but he loves his daughter: that is Jewish, too. Human instincts speak in Jewish bosoms. They know how to love as to hate. As a Jew's portrait, Shylock is accurately painted. What Shakespeare meant in "Merchant of Venice" nobody can tell. Whether he favored Shylock or despised him must remain a secret forever. But he has dowered him with race characteristics and capacity. Shylock is no common man. In Antonio we see the best side out; but those times we saw him, he not knowing we were looking, were in no wise creditable to him. Shylock, on the contrary, has his worst side out. His knife, itching for a pound of flesh nighest Antonio's heart, horrifies us; but all incidental observations of him are in his favor. He has self-respect; he resents the contumely piled upon him like bales upon a beast of burden; though he loves money inordinately (and with reason, seeing it is his sole protection in a civilization hating the Jew as if he were a plague), he loves his daughter too; and, finding she has taken a ring, moans, "It was my turquoise; I had it of Leah when I was a bachelor." Love of money runs into penuriousness as an ultimatum. Jew is come to mean usurer, and not wholly without reason. Shakespeare has given the temper of mediæval Venice toward the Jew. Venice hated, vilified, robbed him when it might, borrowed when it must.

This environment colored Shylock. It educated his worst and dwarfed his best. He became as the trees on the verge of Niagara, twisted, dwarfed, malformed. The winds from the abyss of waters have wrestled with them, buffeted them, till they are distortions. Environment emphasized traits in Shylock, but created none. Shakespeare is exact. Environment is not creative, does not make colors, but simply deepens tints. Shylock's traits are the Jew's traits. Money was his power and safety, but a Jew loves money when safety is not involved. The passion for gold is as old as Abraham. He grew rich. Jacob grew rich while serving for Rachel. Jews are masters of the art of acquiring riches. Antonio hated Shylock; but Shylock hated Antonio. Christianity and Judaism are mutually intolerant, each holding itself custodian of truth; and truth is intolerant, and may easily grow to be browbeating in self-assertiveness. Shylock hated opposition, hated the Gentile. I doubt not he thought the race element in his hatred large, and the individual element insignificant; but this was self-deception. His hunger for revenge was not ethnic, but personal. Shylock would have hid his hate behind impersonality. He was wronged indeed, but wrong as well. Would he had been larger! This is Shylock. He is not himself. He has let adverse circumstances master his nobilities. Thus does he look on the world, a pessimist. "The times are out of joint," and he mistakes Venice for the world. He has not kept face toward God. He has watched Venice, when he should have watched motions of the constellations marching their armies toward God. He miscon-

Shylock and David as Interpreters of Life 335

strued life, because he hated the world. Things, all things were awry, he put down as a foundation truth. We scarcely have it in heart to blame him, his provocation was so great. His world hissed him. Not a friend reached hand toward him in day or dark. He was alone. He was watched as carrion birds, waiting for food, sit by to see a soldier die.

Hear him: "He hath disgraced me, and hindered me half a million; laughed at my losses, mocked at my gains, scorned my nation, thwarted my bargains, cooled my friends, heated mine enemies; and what's his reason? I am a Jew. Hath not a Jew eyes? hath not a Jew hands, organs, dimensions, senses, affections, passions? fed with the same food, hurt with the same weapons, subject to the same diseases, healed by the same means, warmed and cooled by the same winter and summer, as a Christian is? If you prick us, do we not bleed? if you tickle us, do we not laugh? if you poison us, do we not die? if you wrong us, shall we not revenge? If we are like you in the rest, we shall resemble you in that. If a Jew wrong a Christian, what is his humility? revenge. If a Christian wrong a Jew, what should his sufferance be by Christian example? why, revenge. The villainy you teach me, I will execute; and it shall go hard, but I will better the instruction." Clearly, Shylock was bitter, exceeding bitter against the world. Lear was; Timon of Athens was; but the fallacy of pessimism lies here: It bases argument on unsupported propositions. The premises are insufficient. One hypocrite does not justify us treating all men as such. One friend proven untrue, does not prove friendship a delusion. The narrow view is not the true view. One lattice will not give all the heavens. There is a scowl on Shylock's face. It never lifts. He has jaundiced eyes, and white light looks something else; stars have lost brilliancy, and come to be as the spent flame on autumn leaves. Shylock was hostile to life. He was against conditions universal, will war with all, will treat the world as Eric Brighteyes his foes, puts back against the rock, clutches his enemy, hurls him from the cliff, though he and his foe fall to their death together. However natural Shylock's attitude, it was wrong. Life is not to be antagonized, but used; and to become belligerent is to destroy it. To hack with scimiter or crusader's ax is not life eloquent, generative, productive. Shylock was all for venegance, and forgets God's saying, "Vengeance is mine, I will repay." He took his case in his own hands, when righteousness dares leave its case to God. Pessimism blighted Shylock, as it will blight any soul. He was great enough to have kept the color of his own spirit, and not like the sea to have borrowed his hues. Clearly Shylock did not get the right estimate of life.

Contrast Browning's "Saul" with "Merchant of Venice." The poem gives outlook shoreless as the open heavens. Saul, king of Israel, is sunk in lethargy. Coma has seized him. In his darkened tent

"He stood as erect as that tent-prop, both arms stretched out wide
On the great cross-support in the center, that goes on each side;
He relaxed not a muscle, but hung there as caught in his pangs . . .
So agonized Saul, drear and stark, blind and dumb."

And David comes,

"God's child with his dew
On thy gracious gold hair, and those lilies still living and blue,
Just broken to twine round thy harp-strings,
As if no wild heat were raging to torture the desert!"

He "knelt down to the God of his fathers," and rising, begins to play upon his harp. Life sweeps its vision past the poet's eyes. Browning is right; let the poet alone to see. That is his office. He is God's laureate to celebrate God's triumphs and God's truths. A perverted vision sees part; an unhindered vision sees all. Life is one vast circumference, vaster than any of us have guessed. We must allow it growth-room. David is optimist. The air through which he looks is lately washed by rains, so as to be pure. No smoke nor dust hinders sight. Pessimism sees through an imperfect visual medium. Objects are given wrong colors. Imperfect perspectives are conceived. But David looks through serene air. Both near and far are distinct. He gets all objects on the landscape, and gets them in their right relations, a thing so necessary and so difficult. The import of Saul is, Discover, employ, and enjoy life. Let its entirety have a minstry to your spirit. Antagonism of the world, is Shylock; employment of the world, is David.

This is Browning's superior message to his generation. He is little given to complaining.

Complaining is never profitable business. Railing is non-productive. Browning is constructive. Here discover the secret of his might. He is not untangling a skein, but weaving at a loom; his end being not threads, but weft. His question is always

"Why stay we on the earth except to grow?"

Earth, then, is a garden in which we be planted, a space in which to grow and conditions to supply the aliment for growth. Tennyson trusts

"That somehow good
Will be the final goal of ill;"

but Browning is definite. He *knows*. Evil, by antagonisms, does good even here. Neither will he remove its possibility of profit to a remote hereafter. Evil is evil still, but overborne. Hindrances removed or surmounted by our strength give courage, vigor, self-poise, mastery. Here is his teaching Biblical. God did not make evil, but does make "the wrath of man to praise him." Sin is the misuse of free will; and misuse is a prerogative of the free spirit, as is right use. But God is in his world to hinder wrong and help righteousness. The sway of evil is not as appears. Toplady has sung this philosophy thus:

> "But should the surges rise
> And rest delay to come,
> Blest be the tempest, kind the storm
> Which drives us nearer home."

Evil is potent; God is omni-potent. So Browning conceives life as a whole, whose uses are salutary and uplifting. In many poems he presents faces of this truth; in Saul the entire path is trod. From start to goal, nothing is omitted. David is spokesman for life. He begins well:

> "Then I, as was meet
> Knelt down to the God of my fathers."

Prayer is helper to true views. This is a profound fact in the profoundest philosophy. Prayer clarifies air and vision. Then, saith he,

> "I tuned my harp—took off the lilies we twine
>   round its chords,
> Lest they snap 'neath the stress of the noontide—
>   those sunbeams like swords!

> And I first played the tune all our sheep know, as
> one after one
> So docile they come to the pen-door till folding be
> done."

Then the tunes for the birds and the crickets. Then he played "The help-tune of the reapers;" then, "The last song when the dead man is praised on his journey," crooning

> "Bear, bear him along
> With his few faults shut up like dead flowerets."

Nature, the open where birds and flowers are, and

> "Where the long grasses stifle the waters in the stream's bed,"

toil, "the glad chant of marriage," and the solemn chant of death;

> "Then the chorus intoned
> As the Levites go up to the altar in glory enthroned."

Pray what lacks this of being life's procession? No syllable is wanting from the word. Life's music may be free from care, or burdened with toil, or glad with wedding march, or sad with funeral dirge, or solemn with psalm and prayer; for life is all this. But life is a joy, and not a curse to be borne like an o'er-heavy cross.

> "O, the wild joys of living! the leaping from rock
>   up to rock,
>   The strong rending of boughs from the fir-tree,
>   the cool silver shock
>   Of the plunge in a pool's living water, the hunt of
>   the bear,
>   And the sultriness showing the lion is crouched
>   in his lair,
>   And the meal, the rich dates yellowed over with
>   gold-dust divine,
>   And the locust-flesh steeped in the pitcher, the
>   full draught of wine,
>   And the sleep in the dried river-channel where
>   bulrushes tell
>   That the water was wont to go warbling so softly
>   and well.
>
>   How good is man's life, the mere living! how fit
>   to employ
>   All the heart and the soul and the senses forever
>   in joy!
>   Hast thou loved the white locks of thy father,
>   whose sword thou did'st guard
>   When he trusted thee forth with the armies, for
>   glorious reward?

Did'st thou see the thin hands of thy mother, held
    up as men sung
The low song of the nearly departed, and hear her
    faint tongue
Joining in while it could to the witness, 'Let one
    more attest
I have lived, seen God's hand through a lifetime,
    and all was for best!'"

Who does not recognize this as true? The bounding step, the resiliency of youth, the cloudless hope, the joy in mere physical existence, the delight in simple life, in whose air birds carol and flowers grow beautiful! Ecstasy is on us. The laughter and singing of little children is native to them as babbling and brightness to the brooks. There is a sheer, unreasoning laughter of spirit, and a muscular delight whose rejoicing is in existence as strong men in triumph of battle. You are eager for life, as a fair woman for her lover's coming. The world is bounteous in beauty. Flowers and clouds and landscapes and fair women are God's visible æsthetics. "Enjoy the day," sang epicurean Horace; and he was right, if we may put an interpretation on his words. Enjoy the world. It is a fountain spouting waters in summer from a precipice of snow, cold, crystal clear, intoxicating to the eye, limpid as a good man's soul, and a sheer delight to parched lips,—drink and be glad! Let your soul laugh, like sunbeams kissing flowers. Recall the beauty of New England hills. The climbing mountain, the blue far vistas, the music-murmur of pines, the drift of slow clouds across your plot of surprising azure, the sagging meadow, tall with grasses, and the brooks,—who can tell of them as they are? The noisy stream coming from hidden sources, bustling, busy, intent, going racing toward the sea,—how the waters hurry round the pebbles, how they visit old and gnarly tree-roots, and gather in a pool pellucid as light where the fish lie aslumber at noon; how it laves the mosses and catches reluctant pine-cones and bears them as freight on its rocking tide! Like a cheerful face, the brook's smile is for everything. It has no favorites. Little children or solemn kine may stand in its clear waters. It can not wait, but wild with glee dances down the mountain-side. How wild the laughter of it! How its voices tangle with our dreams! How it bids everybody "Be glad, be glad!" How it stands in deep hollows, and rests as if grown weary with its racing, then eddies and spurts, and good-bye—and is gone down and on, and yonder sings its way into a river, and the river babbles over its stones and rushes down rapids in foam and tangle and silver, and leaps in a waterfall; and all the night you sleep with the waters singing like some serenader at your window, and your dreams are helped as by an unseen angel's singing. Or on a sunny day, lie in the meadows, and listen to hidden waters where beneath grasses they find a tortuous channel. But for the voice you would not know a thread of stream passed near you. But push grasses aside, and see how a chalice full of crystal reflects your face, and into it, as some mimic silver chimes soft and sweet as voices of our beloved, a stream is falling. Who can forget these voices of the hidden waters? Or who can deny life has delight, when such memories haunt the mind's daylight and dark? But life is more, always more. God knows where all life is, but we get it by fragments as children get knowledge. 'T is a long though delightsome voyage to circumnavigate this sea. Life is ample as eternity. Beginnings alone are here. Life is enjoying; but life is also achieving.

To lie by brooklets, dreaming in the sun, is not life at its best. We are to do. We are parts of history. We come and pass, but leave a shadow and a footprint where we trod. We change the world we came to. And so this poet David must strike harp to sing kingship now:

"Each deed thou hast done
Dies, revives, goes to work in the world until e'en as the sun
Looking down on the earth, though clouds spoil him, though tempests efface,
Can find nothing his own deed produced not, must everywhere trace
The results of his past summer-prime,—so, each ray of thy will,
Every flash of thy passion and prowess, long over, shall thrill
Thy whole people, the countless, with ardor, until they, too, bring forth
A like cheer to their sons; who in turn fill the South and the North
With the audience thy deed was the germ of. Carouse in the past!"

And he thrills the dreaming spirit to the point of march, conquest, enthronement. Our long to-day is arena where power struggles and achieves. Make self a prince, a mighty memory on whose wings the ages shall be upborne. Achieve! Life is more than playground. It is harvest-field and battle-field. It is a place to suffer and bear silent sorrow, and exert the effort of a Hercules, and know the prose of toil and poetry of battle. All life is, live! Edward Rowland Sill is right:

"Forenoon and afternoon and night,—Forenoon,
And afternoon, and night,—forenoon and—what!
The empty song repeats itself. No more?

Yea, that is life: make this forenoon sublime,
This afternoon a psalm, this night a prayer,
And Time is conquered, and thy crown is won."

Enduring is itself conquest. All that asserts the mastery of man over environment and his own conscious and necessary regality are to be set down in the column of achievement. To think, to become transcendent, to defy spaces and geographies, to use stars as lamps to light us on our journey, to hold communion with immortals, be they poets, philosophers, generals, discoverers, seers, to feel the vigor of creation on us, and become "makers" as poets are, to feel that all human achievements lie at our feet like waves breaking on a shore,—to think. And this is a territory of the domain of life. Here men become equals. Here riches and birth become tawdry. Here centuries meet as brothers. This is the democracy of thought, and thought is achievement splendid and immortal.

But living, enjoying, achieving, is that life's circumference? By man's philosophy it may be, but by a Divine philosophy it is not. Love is left yet, and God and these make life complete. A poet says:

> "Love maketh life and life's great work complete.
>   Some day will come the setting of the sun,
>   And this brief day of the long work be done.
> There will be folded hands, lips without breath;
>   But we shall have passed on—love knows no death."

Love is greater than achieving. Conquest may be for self, and often is; but love is always for others. Let Saul rise to love. Let his conquests become subsidiary.

But—God! He is life's goal.

> "Then the truth came upon me. No harp more—
>   No song more! outbroke"—

And God burst on the soul! I climbed a mountain of the Sierras. The way was steep; the boulders were huge, the pines stood marshaled like troops of soldiers, when, on a sudden, I found me on a height; and a lake bluer than skies of Italy filled all my field of view. The background was snowy peaks, and the hollow filled to the brim with a wonder of blue waters. I saw nothing else. This seized my senses. Thus David caught sight of God. Moral truth made his landscape. God swallowed up all besides. He was blinded by it, and broke off his music. When God is seen, who shall attempt song or harp?

"I have gone the whole round of creation: I saw and I spoke;
I a work of God's hand for that purpose, received in my brain,
And pronounced on the rest of his handiwork— returned him again
His creation's approval or censure: I spoke as I saw.
I report as a man may of God's work—all's love, yet all's law.
Now I lay down the judgeship he lent me. Every faculty tasked
To perceive him, has gained an abyss, where a dew-drop was asked.
Have I knowledge? Confounded it shrivels at Wisdom laid bare.
Have I forethought? How purblind, how blank to the Infinite Care!

> Do I task any faculty highest to image success?
> I but open my eyes,—and perfection, no more and no less,
> In the kind I imagined, full-fronts me, and God is seen God
> In the star, in the stone, in the flesh, in the soul and the clod.
> And thus looking within and around me, I ever renew
> (With that stoop of the soul which in bending upraises it too)
> The submission of man's nothing-perfect to God's all-complete,
> As by each new obeisance of spirit I climb to his feet."
>
> "I seek and find it. O Saul, it shall be
> A face like my face that receives thee; a man like to me,
> Thou shalt love and be loved by, forever; a Hand like this hand
> Shall throw open the gates of new life to thee! See the Christ stand!"

So "Saul" sets, a blaze of glory.

And who is right, Shylock or David? Life is antagonism, Shylock said. Life is being, enjoying, enduring, suffering, thinking, achieving, believing, loving, seeing God and getting Christ, said David. David is right. Life is not so much exclusion as inclusion. And as the horizon holds hill, valley, hamlet, solitude, woodland, sunrise, and sunset, home with little children and God's quiet acre,—so life contains ourselves, from the mere joy of living, through loving, up to mighty joy of holding God by the right hand so we shall not be moved. This is David's amazing estimate; and it assures the spirit, answers our deepest need, gives wings and might, courage and conquest; and calms our unrest,

> "Like the benediction
> That follows after prayer."

An Angel Came

One noon I met an angel by the way,
And giving hand of welcome, bade him stay
      Beneath my roof and rest.
He looked aweary, having traveled far;
From heaven he came, in that remoter star
Than men have mapped on the celestial sphere.
With grave, sweet face, he stood. His voice was clear
      As silver bells. He dressed
In mystic, seamless garment, dyed with blood;
And round him, glory whitened like a flood
Of morning light. My home with many a guest,
Brave men and pure, had oftentime been blessed;
      But now,—an angel stood
Tall and compassionate, beneath my roof!
At heart, I thought, "How shall I give him proof
That he is welcome?" "This home," I said,
"Is thine. Wait thou until the heat be fled,
      And by the stream and wood
Cool shadows gather. Angel, be my guest,
Sit thou in quietude and take thy rest."

"My name is—" "Nay," the gracious angel said,
"Thy name is known in heaven;" and then he fled
Swift like the light across the ample sea,
But left an angel at my heart with me.

www.ingramcontent.com/pod-product-compliance
Lightning Source LLC
Chambersburg PA
CBHW032354230426
43672CB00007B/701